THE ART OF
Speaking
Into Existence

GLENN BOWIE

Publishing

THE ART OF
Speaking Into Existence
by Glenn Bowie

Published by GBS Publishing

Publishing

Cover Design and Photography by Karen Floyd

Interior Book Design and Typography by Lea Frechette

Edited by Jed Wolfe

Softback ISBN: 978-1-0879-1418-3

Softback first edition 2020

Printed in the United States of America
10 9 8 7 6 5 4 3 2 1 0

Glenn Bowie Speaks, Inc.
254 N. Lake Ave #300
Pasadena, CA 91101

Visit us online at glennbowiespeaks.com

TABLE OF CONTENTS

DEDICATION

I dedicate this book to the woman who laid the foundation for my life, which was built on her unlimited faith, unchanging heart, grace, and determination. The structure, Alice Bowie, still stands. Under her council and guidance, I have been able to live my life by example.

I am a witness to life in the projects, where I was content growing up with my family to lean on as a means of survival. Mom then positioned our family in middle-class America, which was a pivotal period in my life that opened my mind to different cultures and races. There is good and bad in all people. We must give everyone a fair chance and never judge by appearance.

Mom molded me to be the best I can be by staying true to myself. She shaped my values by helping me to know who I am and accept myself, by knowing my strengths, passions, limits, and purpose in life. She encouraged me to live my life by helping someone else without expecting anything in return, in order to make the world a better place.

Thank you, mom.

Glenn

ACKNOWLEDGEMENTS

Thank you God for all your blessings and guidance throughout my life.

Thank you to Lisa Polnitz, Daphna Levy, Lea Frechette, Jed Wolfe, and Char Webster for all your help in getting this book project started and completed. To Blair Underwood, John Combs and Gus Blackmon for your inspiration and heartfelt words. To Karen Floyd Photography for making me look good on my cover photo. To Herb Hunter for my first sales job and believing in me.

To my dad Lawrence Bowie and my mom Alice Bowie for bringing me into this world.

A special thank you to my brothers Larry and Charles who helped pave the way for me and were instrumental in my growth, and to my sister René who encouraged me to reach for my dreams.

Thank you to all my family and friends which is a long list that could go on and on....

I appreciate and love you all.

FOREWORD

I met Glenn Bowie more than twenty years ago as a maverick and "rising star" in the mobile tech industry. *The Art of Speaking Into Existence* by Glenn Bowie is a testimony to what can happen if you walk in the path of your purpose. He lets you know that you *can* triumph if you stay true to yourself and the values instilled in you.

"Bowie-Bowie"* speaks boldly into existence a life without limits through his determination and will to succeed. Open your mind to receive from this book the "art of desire." Glenn's desire to dream big has paid off and now he is paying it forward.

Glenn, thanks for being there for my family and me throughout the years.

Blair Underwood

---

*"Bowie-Bowie" is a nickname that was given to Glenn by Blair Underwood.

INTRODUCTION

AMERICA'S FOUNDING FATHERS DID SOMETHING EXCEPTIONAL WHICH HAS BEEN AT THE FOUNDATION OF OUR COUNTRY'S SUCCESS. Rather than reinforcing different classes of people or encouraging everyone to be the same (socialism), they created what we call the American Dream. They felt the country would be better off if all the citizens were given the freedom either to be all they could be, or to not succeed, in their chosen direction.

This simple principle has made such an important difference in the success of our country (versus other countries based on different philosophies): the amazing companies that have been dominating the world markets, the high-paying jobs created, and the personal satisfaction of knowing that we can achieve anything we set our minds to. Glenn Bowie is the best example I know of delivering on the American Dream!

The very best teacher of the core principles of success that I know was Earl Nightingale, in his *Lead the Field* series. In his principles, Mr. Nightingale says: "Your rewards in life will always match your service." While I didn't learn this principle until I was in my late twenties and Glenn's mother may never have heard of Earl Nightingale, she had instilled this incredibly powerful gift deep in Glenn's soul: "Don't focus on your rewards, focus on service to others, and the rewards will follow." This principle is as undeniably true as the physical laws of nature (i.e., gravity, electricity flow, speed of light, etc.).

Glenn's sales accomplishments are much too numerous and distinguished to try to list here. You are going to have to read the book. Glenn was the salesperson who set the example for others to follow with his extraordinary sales performance, so much so that at Nextel we created a special award, the "Making It Happen" award. Glenn was Nextel's top producing sales executive in the Southwest Area. As the top producer, we wanted him to receive some special recognition.

Of all the recognition award ceremonies I have attended over my career, his was the most emotional. What made this so special was the character of the winner. Glenn didn't get to be number 1 out of 150 sales executives by outworking them or clawing someone out of his way. He did it by serving his customers, gaining their trust, and enlisting their help to grow his business.

If you ask Glenn for his secret to success, it won't be hard work, discipline, commitment, or positive attitude, although he possesses them all. It would be that he was blessed to understand that showing grace and serving others works!

John Combs
Former President Nextel Communications Southwest Area

"YOUR REWARDS IN LIFE WILL ALWAYS MATCH YOUR SERVICE."

— EARL NIGHTINGALE

CHAPTER ONE

Growing Up
in the Projects

Growing Up in the Projects

RICHARD PRYOR AND I HAVE SOMETHING IN COMMON. We both started our lives in poverty-stricken parts of Peoria, Illinois.

It's true, my life began in poverty, but life today is all about prosperity. I learned early on that where one starts does not necessarily dictate where one finishes. Creating the life of my dreams was based on specific lessons learned over time and put into practice. What made the difference for me can also make the difference for you.

Our family was bonded to the soul of the matriarch, my mother, Alice Bowie. She had a clear, indestructible vision to prepare her children to be the best they could be. Mom always found a way out of "no way" because she lived by faith. She instilled these ideals in each of us kids as a foundation for building our character and values.

After divorcing my alcoholic dad, mom moved our family to the Taft Homes Housing Projects where I was born. I had three older siblings, Larry, Charles, and René. As a single, divorced mother raising four children, life was extremely difficult in those early years. My mom worked three jobs to keep food on the table in a tiny apartment housing the five of us. Adding to obvious stresses, the state of Illinois was contemplating the separation of our family. I remember always hanging on to mom at the front door as she was leaving for work, wondering if she was ever going to come back home.

I loved to be around the older folks. I listened to their stories and then drew my own conclusions as to what I would do in similar circumstances. I thought being a good listener would help me figure out what I wanted in life and what I needed to avoid.

Listening to and observing others was one way I used to create a vision for my future.

FAITH AND FAMILY

Church played a big part in our lives. My grandpa, T.B. Bush, was a Deacon for over fifty years at Mount Zion Baptist Church. My grandma, Esther Bush, served as a soloist, and as Choir Director and Minister of Music. Once grandpa and grandma heard about the state threatening to separate our family, they took on the task of helping to raise and shape us into the people we are today.

We attended church every Sunday. Mom insisted that Larry, Charles, and I dress our best for church. My wardrobe included a suit and tie, and René's attire would always include a pretty dress. Mom instilled in us the idea that we needed to look our best. "You never get a second chance to make a first impression," she would say.

My brother Charles would rebel because he did not want to wear a tie or a sports coat. Mom would ask, "Charles, where is your sports coat? Where is your tie?"

Charles would argue. Occasionally, I succeeded in making peace. I'd say to him, "Just wear the tie to make mom happy. Church will only last a few hours."

DRESSED FOR SUCCESS

I loved wearing a suit and tie. I always wanted to look my best. I sat in the congregation with my grandpa and the other church deacons when I was about five, the first time I ever saw men together in black suits and ties. I thought it was cool, sitting there like I was a deacon myself. That's where I earned my nickname, "Deek."

At the end of the service, the deacons would count the money. They would make sure all the bills were paid and that anyone in need of groceries, clothes, or rent got help. I called them the Care Givers of the church.

Music was a big part of church life as well as our family life. My oldest brother Larry played piano and organ for the church. That was something you had to experience. He played so well it made me proud. Grandpa was a ragtime piano player, and mom was in a group called "The Bush Trio" with her sisters, Alva and Vivian. They sang in the choir and performed in other places in the Peoria area. My uncle Charles, for whom my brother was named, played saxophone.

I was timid so mom thought it would be a good idea to get me involved in the children's choir and expose me to the audience of the church. She signed me up to be in the Christmas and Easter plays. She hoped getting me involved in activities would break my shyness. This exposure opened my mind to experiences that shaped my character.

I was baptized at Mount Zion Baptist Church and gave my life to Christ at a young age. I looked forward to getting submerged in waist-deep water for the forgiveness of sins and officially becoming a member of the church. But I made a mistake that turned this special moment into one of the biggest embarrassments of my life. On that day, I wore my best Sunday suit. However, I had forgotten a change of clothes so I had to be baptized in my underwear. Better to be baptized in my underwear than get my Sunday suit wet.

BAPTISM

On that same day my uncle, Reverend R. Wendell Phillips, baptized a very large gentleman and accidentally dropped him in the water. The poor fellow hit his head on the back of the tub, which made a loud noise. The entire congregation was surprised into laughter. My uncle had a hard time getting him up. I thought he was going to drown. It was scary until a couple of deacons got there in time to get the gentleman out of the water.

I was glad I had gotten to go first and wasn't dropped. The experience was incredible: the Holy Spirit overtook my body. Getting baptized is a beautiful and spiritual experience. My grandmother always said, "Invite Jesus Christ into your heart."

Communion was on the first Sunday of every month. We enjoyed the taste of the fresh grape juice and the crackers which represented the body and blood of Jesus Christ. After church, we headed downstairs to the church basement, trying to beat the crowd and get the leftover juice and crackers. Even today, I still love juice and crackers. Mom always knew where to find us after church.

There was nothing like the occasional chicken dinners we had in the church basement after the service to raise money for the building fund. Being young I would think to myself, "Why do we need building funds? The church is already built!"

SUNDAYS

Grandma baked a cake every week and had a Sunday dinner feast ready for the family after church. On Sundays I always spent time talking with grandpa. After a few minutes, he would say, "Go on back there and visit with your grandma." He knew I liked spending time with grandma in the kitchen where all the food was cooking.

Grandpa and grandma also invited those less fortunate to come and have a good meal after church service. When a guest would come over it had a positive effect on me because it led me to appreciate our life and how blessed we were. But at the same time I thought to myself, "No leftovers this weekend to take home."

I loved making people laugh, especially since my grandpa was so serious. I felt proud when grandma told me I was the only one in the family who could make grandpa laugh. The problem was that sometimes I didn't know how to stop.

My sister René and I had a standing ritual at mealtime. In the middle of our grandpa's extensive prayer, we would open our eyes, look at each other, and then look at all the food on the table. We took in the aroma with enjoyment. It was so strong that one time while everyone's eyes were closed, I tried to sneak a piece of pie. I reached my arm out across the table towards the pie. Smack! Grandma slapped me on the back of my head. Her fingers were so heavy that it felt like a hammer had hit me in the head. That was the end of that ritual.

It took grandpa a long time to bless the food. Maybe it was just me, but the prayer seemed really long. Then grandma made us learn a Bible verse. I used the same one every Sunday. Grandma would tell me, "You can do better," and "Learn another." I felt bad until I looked around the corner and saw mom quickly turning Bible pages getting ready for her turn.

A SAFE AUDIENCE

As a good listener, I always "tuned in" to my uncle, the Reverend R. Wendell Phillips, during every service. I would go home after church and imitate my uncle. I did it so much that the family thought I was going to be a preacher. I would have a handkerchief in my hand, climb up on my mother's washer, and set my Bible up on top of the refrigerator in the kitchen as my pulpit. At six years old, I imitated my uncle while the family listened and laughed. I liked putting smiles on their faces and joy in their hearts. Eventually my mom would say, "That's enough, now get down." I could have gone on for hours if she had let me.

To this day, my faith is what keeps me going. I walk and stand on my faith. Through generational blessings, built on family structure, I am blessed. My grandpa, grandma, and mom made it easier for those of us that came after them. I will never let their sacrifices go to waste. The grace they stored up for future generations must live on.

Without family structure, one could lose their way. My family is my foundation and a place to return to when things go wrong. I can go to anyone in my family for help and things will fall right back into place. I want to be that kind of mentor for someone who could use a big brother or needs someone to talk to. Not everyone has a family to rely on for support.

From observing others and listening carefully, I realized early on that life is what you make it. Through my mother's example, in particular, I came to understand that I had a choice to look beyond my situation and to believe that I could achieve my goals and dreams.

LIFE IS EXACTLY WHAT YOU MAKE IT. GO FOR YOUR DREAMS!

CHAPTER TWO

A Pact

CHAPTER TWO

A PACT

I WAS INSPIRED BY CALVIN, MY BROTHER LARRY'S BIRD. He was confined to a cage, and I was confined to a small apartment in the projects.

I had dreams of being free. To me, birds symbolize freedom, hope, and desire. I wanted to spread my wings one day and reach greater heights. At that point in my life, I constructed a vision board that I taped to my bedroom's plaster wall. I attached pictures of anything that could reach a higher plane in this life — things like eagles, hawks, and airplanes. I dreamed big and shared my thoughts with my mom. She came in at times to look at my vision board to see how it had grown. Mom told me to think outside of the box — Calvin's cage, our apartment, the projects — and follow my dreams.

I also shared my dreams and vision with my brother Charles. One day he told me that he too was looking for a way out. He said, "Why do you think I'm involved with sports? It's a way out, and I am a different person when

I'm on the football field or the basketball court." Charles and I shook hands and made a pact that we would always support each other's dreams. I liked having Charles as a mentor and father figure in my life. We both made valuable contributions to each other over time.

At Irving Primary School, Charles was on the basketball team, and I was the team mascot for the Irving Bulldogs. I liked being a mascot. It was my first introduction to sports.

We also had basketball tournaments in our bedroom using a rubber ball and a homemade basketball rim between our bunk beds. We would invite a bunch of neighborhood kids over to join in the game. Charles and my relationship grew closer with shared interests.

One day before a big game, Charles looked all through our room to find a pair of socks. He couldn't find any, so I opened my piggy bank and gave him money to buy a fresh pair.

I had watched my mom manage finances and knew saving money was an intricate part of reaching her dreams, so I had saved as well. I learned about sharing that day, and it also taught Charles how important it is to save money. He ran to the store and arrived with the socks just in time for the game.

A DAY IN THE LIFE

My mom's vision to optimize her kids' lives led her to create experiences and learning opportunities for us. She was always in action, doing what it took, no matter what.

There were many hot days when mom watched the neighborhood kids play while sitting on the porch. In those days, you felt safe playing outside until the streetlights came on. So we played kickball in the big field near home until almost sundown.

When mom was ready to call us in for the night, she'd stroll down to the big field. She'd say, "Don't you see the streetlights are on? That means playtime is over." Larry and René would run towards home. Charles and I always wanted to play longer. To get our attention, mom acted as if she had a megaphone and yelled, "Playtime is over!" Every child who was playing kickball would stop and go home. During those days, what one parent said was good enough for all the kids on the block.

Mom worked three jobs to keep food on the table and the bills paid. Her favorite job was as a DJ at radio station WPEO. She brought records home from the radio station and played them for us kids.

René and I danced together for family entertainment. We practiced our dance moves to James Brown, Al Green, the Temptations, Diana Ross and the Supremes, etc. Mom would invite her girlfriends or a few ladies from church to come over for a visit, and she'd call René and me downstairs to dance together for them.

We hustled tips, but mom made us give all the money back. We stayed standing at the bottom of the stairway, waiting for mom to turn her back and go into the kitchen. When she did, the ladies would give us the money back, and we would run upstairs to count it. During the 1960s, a couple of dollars was a lot of candy money. Everything was a penny, so you could get one hundred pieces of candy for a dollar.

Mom loved basketball. As a DJ she got to meet the Bradley Braves, our town college basketball team. She had house parties for such Bradley University basketball players as Chet "The Jet" Walker, Alex McNutt, and Joe Strawder, to name a few. Bradley had a winning team at that time, and Bradley basketball undoubtedly "Played in Peoria."

They all came by the apartment after the basketball games and listened to music, played cards, and danced with the family. Mom served Pepsi and peanuts that she special-ordered from The Nut House in downtown

Peoria. She prepared a home-cooked meal for the team to make them feel right at home. Such nights were among the highlights of my childhood.

My mom taught me that a vision — the end result one is seeking — is manifested more quickly by visualizing the details. For me that included using a vision board, sharing my dreams with others, making a pact with someone holding a similar vision, and being consistent in action towards reaching goals.

VISUALIZING YOUR DREAMS CREATES ENERGY AND PURPOSE.

CHAPTER THREE

A LEAP OF FAITH

A Leap of Faith

MY TEENS WERE FORMATIVE YEARS, WHERE I LEARNED VALUABLE LESSONS. I was faced with serious challenges, opportunities, and experiences to try new things.

I remember going house-hunting with mom. She wanted a house close to a school, away from the dangers of the river, so we could play and be safe. It also had to be something she could afford. That's how we landed at 905 E. Tripp Street. It was a tiny house, less than 1,000 square feet for the five of us.

We were the only black family on the block. On the day we moved in, all of our neighbors came out and stood on their front lawns staring in disbelief as we unloaded our furniture. I was staring at the basketball rim attached to a neighbor's garage, imagining shooting long-range baskets with new friends. While mom had a vision to better our lives, my goal was to build relationships to better enjoy my life.

Mom knew you could win people over with kindness and respect. She instructed us to wave and smile, to go over and introduce ourselves. Over time, we were able to break the barrier and got to know our neighbors.

VON STEUBEN GRADE SCHOOL

I attended Von Steuben Grade School, a couple of blocks from home. René and I walked down the street to school and through the athletic field every day, which seemed like miles away to me as a kid. It was scary in the beginning, starting a new school and forging new friendships, but I kept an open mind. Mom always told us a smile would go a long way.

After getting settled in, I got to know the Hubers, who lived directly across the street. One day, I was sitting on the porch staring at their son Dave, who was out shooting baskets. He waved me over, inviting me to play basketball on his court — I felt like I'd died and gone to heaven. Dave was my age and had an older brother, Jim, who was the same age as my brother Charles. The rivalry began, and it was brothers against brothers in basketball, corkball, baseball and football.

I got a chance to see other types of family structures from our neighbors. For example, I didn't like that right in the middle of a heated basketball game, Dave and Jim would have to stop at 5 p.m. for dinner every day. By then

Charles and I would be up by twenty points anyway, but at our house you ate whenever you got hungry. Maybe I would have gotten used to their custom sooner if we were invited in for dinner. We finally accepted this different lifestyle, knowing we would finish the game later.

After a while, Jim wanted to switch up the teams to make up for the fact that they kept losing. We had to break up our brotherly team or risk not playing at all. Charles and I looked at each other, smiled, and agreed.

Eventually, we would head down to the Von Steuben playground in search of a full-court basketball game and stiffer competition. We invited Dave and Jim to join us. Our friendship grew, and I had my buddy Dave at least until 5 p.m. It taught me that I had to respect the time schedule of others.

JUST MY IMAGINATION, RUNNING AWAY WITH ME

I formed a group called The Dynamic Three. I was the lead singer. My friends Bryant and Robert were the other two members. We patterned ourselves after the Temptations, and I practiced every day at mom's house. After some time, we decided to sign up for the talent show at Von Steuben Grade School.

The big night came, and boy did we put on a show. The noise from the crowd escalated. The lights came up as the crowd chanted, "Dynamic Three, Dynamic Three!" We stood with our backs to the audience. Our adrenaline was flowing. As soon as the curtain opened, the crowd roared. We spun around as the music came on and moved in sync as we sang the Temptations' "Just My Imagination (Running Away with Me)." We won second place, and it was an experience that had me thinking of going into show business.

Life was changing for the better, but mom always reminded us never to forget where we came from. It was my first experience with getting to know other cultures and races, and I welcomed it with open arms.

Around this time, I learned I had a competitive spirit. In our neighborhood, my friends and I would ride our bikes. My bike, "The Bus," bought by my aunt Alva for my birthday, helped me win long-distance races. I would build up speed and then coast past the other kids. After a race one day I thought, "It's not how you start the race, but how you finish."

As I was growing up, I never stopped adding to my vision board. By the time I was a teenager, my board was filled with pictures, inspirational words, quotes, and thoughts that represented my experiences, feelings, and what I wanted to "speak into existence." I was clear that speaking something into existence isn't just about being clear on goals and sharing them with others, it was about doing the work it takes to earn the end result. Most things do not just happen out of nowhere. The majority of what it would take to reach my goals would require me to take conscious, consistent actions and the help of others.

Musicians and sports figures were my inspiration. Reggie Jackson, a famous baseball player, inspired me to play baseball. I loved soulful rhythm and blues groups. I had pictures of California plastered on my vision board. I knew one day I would go there. I posted pictures from the Rose Bowl and the Rose Parade in sunny Pasadena, California. The mountains seemed to call my name. Eventually, as an adult, I moved there.

PLAY BALL

Baseball was a team sport, but individually you could contribute to the team's success. Baseball taught me that sometimes you have to make a sacrifice to advance the runner to get them in scoring position. There is a strategy on each play, and the end result is to score as many runs as it takes to win the game. I received my very first Little League trophy during that period. I may have received the trophy, but without my teammates it would not have been possible. I realized that life is a team effort. It taught me that I should look for mentors that not only discussed baseball, but real life situations too. I learned that I could not make it on my own. I had to get direction from the coach and make quick decisions, which was easier on a baseball diamond than in life. In real life I like to think things over and not rush decisions. Most of the bad decisions I made in life were rushed.

FULL COURT PRESS

Sports continued to play a big role in my life. I tried out for the basketball team and played for the Von Steuben Vikings. I started at point guard position and triumphed when our team won two city championships.

I would practice dribbling my rubber ball down the hallway in our house to the beat of the Bradley Braves' fight song. It was running through my head over and over again. Each entryway to a room was my make-believe basketball rim. René followed right behind me, cheering me on all the way.

I remember when Von Steuben played Longfellow grade school and we beat them 79 to 1. Longfellow only made one free throw the whole game. Then came the time when Von Steuben played against Irving, my old school. I knew most of the players on the team because they lived in the Taft Homes Housing Projects (the projects where I had begun), and it felt like a homecoming game.

Dave Miller was my first basketball coach. He taught me things not just about the game of basketball but about life. He felt that if you were in the best physical shape you could outlast the other team in the end. He ran us and practice was tough. He taught strategy and instilled in us the importance of scoring.

This was great advice against Irving, since Irving had one of the best pressure defenses in the city. In the championship game against Irving, we were down by 20 points at halftime. Coach took his clipboard and broke it over a locker. He told us that if we lost this game he was going to run us until our tongues fell out in practice. We came out for the second half and won in double overtime! That taught me to never give up, no matter the circumstances.

I enjoyed getting my teammates involved. We had a bunch of great players. They each understood their role. Two years later, we won the city championship again. Coach Miller instilled confidence in the team that we could win and that we should believe in each other and play team basketball. He was a sound fundamentals coach who believed in us. We trusted his guidance.

WOODRUFF HIGH SCHOOL

By the time I got to high school, Larry and Charles had graduated. Larry had become a music teacher at the school. René and I rode the school bus together. She was a junior and I was a freshman. She was on the cheerleading squad and had a passion for hair and make-up. Becoming a "Woodruff Warrior" was inspirational and intriguing. It made me proud to attend school, and it didn't hurt having other family members who had paved the way.

Freshman year at Woodruff was all about playing baseball and basketball. They were my driving purposes. Academics were not my focus. I thought street smarts were better than book smarts. High school was like a playground, an escape. I liked seeing all my friends from the Taft Homes who were with me at Woodruff. It felt like an extension of Irving and Von Steuben.

There was a little envy from some of them because mom had moved our family out of the projects. But once they learned my character and found I was the same person they had known in the Taft Homes, there was no friction, and the negativity turned into positive relationships. I was always proud to be from the Taft Homes and enjoyed meeting new friends from Von Steuben, so I was open to growing and developing as a person.

My coach, Mr. Fogelsong, was a good father figure. He mentored me. He always asked me if I needed socks, spikes or gloves when I played baseball. We would practice in the gym. He would hit ground balls so hard that I knew if I could field his ground balls, I could handle any team's ground balls. I had a competitive spirit, and it came out when I played shortstop all four years of high school.

High school went by fast. I had continued to participate in baseball and basketball as my main focus, but eventually warmed up to the idea of studying. I began to learn from others, ask questions, and honestly apply myself. On weekends I worked at the car wash and earned twenty dollars each day, Saturday and Sunday. Mom told me to save ten dollars every payday, and over time, it would grow. Saving has been a part of my master plan ever since.

My dreams have been actualized by first being clear on what they were. For example, I knew that I wanted a life beyond what seemed available in my hometown. By creating and continually adding to my vision board, I became clearer on what end results appealed to me. This allowed me to be in action, to gain experience and seek mentors towards my goals.

Being consistently in action is one of the keys to success. A person has to take part in and take responsibility for their dreams, and if done correctly and with passion, I can wholeheartedly say that they deserve what they have wished for.

BE IN ACTION!

CHAPTER FOUR

LIFE WITH DAD

LIFE WITH DAD

ALTHOUGH AN ABSENTEE FATHER, my dad was still influential in shaping my thoughts and choices.

It's not that I never saw my father when I was little, just not very much. Until I was about ten, I saw him once a month or so. During some of those early visits, dad would sit around with his friends and play cards. I would stand, watch, and listen.

One time one of my dad's friends said in a critical tone, "Lawrence, your son's just staring at us while we play cards. What's wrong with him?" Dad responded with true grit in his voice, "Let me tell you something about my son. He's listening and learning. He is listening to every word we're saying. Don't think he's not."

I smiled at my dad's friend and walked away, surprised and proud that my dad knew me so well. My intent was to learn the game. And as with most learning, watching and listening expedites the lesson much more quickly than talking.

I remember times when my dad had a mouse in his house. Typically, he would call me and say with fear in his voice, "Come over. There is something in the kitchen. Come quick!" If I didn't get to his house fast enough, he called me again. "I just need you to get here, son. There is something behind the oven."

When I got to his house, he was standing there, shaking, with a drink in one hand and a cigarette in the other. I looked behind the oven and found a mouse the size of my pinky finger and disposed of it. I turned to my dad and said, "Weren't you a Golden Gloves boxer? Didn't you grow up in the streets and learn how to take care of yourself? How can you be scared of a little mouse?" Dad, still anxious, replied, "Those things make me nervous."

It was the alcohol talking through my dad, and it let me know that no matter how big and strong you are as a person, we all have strengths and weaknesses. I had to focus on his strengths, which were productive and positive conversations early in the evenings.

As the night went on, I thought about how blessed I was that I wasn't constantly exposed to the environment he had created. It made me appreciate each day and consider what I wanted and did not want for my life. Whenever I needed to talk to my dad about something, I had to visit him by early evening when he was coherent. My dad's situation taught me to focus on my strengths or things I needed to improve.

Dad lived on Fourth Street, right across from Sheridan Road (later renamed Richard Pryor Place). When I was in high school, I always went to my dad's house on Saturday evenings and banged on the door.

I knew that by evening on Saturday, Mr. Bailey would have delivered catfish in a small plastic bag containing about ten pieces that he sold for ten dollars. Dad would fry the catfish, and we would also have pasta. Then we'd sit back and talk about life.

My dad loved to boil his food, but catfish was the only time I would see him frying with hot grease. He ate healthy most of the time, and that's what helped keep him alive. He was practical from that perspective. We had good times talking about my vision and goals, and I listened to his military stories. I left his house realizing that my dad didn't have any goals or burning desires to improve his situation. That was something I did not want for my life.

My dad helped introduce me to sports. He loved Joe Louis and pretended to be him. I saw holes in the plaster walls at his place and knew he had been sparring. Dad and his brother, Joe Bowie, were both Golden Gloves winners in the Peoria area. His goal to be a great boxer ended when he broke his nose.

I remember picking him up and driving him to my mom's house occasionally to watch Mike Tyson fight. My goal was to get dad out of his environment and see another way of living, which I knew could help change his perspective. But sometimes Tyson fights would be over fast because he would knock the opponent out in the first round!

Dad gave me the gift of my first car, a 1968 Chevrolet Impala. After my experiences with the car, I realized that life is not always perfect. However, it doesn't mean that you are settling for less. You see, the driver's side door had a dent in it, making getting in and out of the car a real challenge. I had to slide into the driver seat from the passenger side.

My friends and neighbors laughed at me when they saw me in that car, but I had the last laugh. In wintertime, when it was forty below zero, the neighbors could not start their cars. My Impala would fire right up. I would smile and wave back at them, sitting in the warmth of the car's heater.

I stopped by to visit my dad when I came home from school once and noticed that his neighborhood had taken a serious turn for the worse. As I walked up to the front porch, I saw a bunch of unfamiliar people on the sidewalk drinking and partying. Things were not right. I banged on my dad's apartment door.

Comrade was my dad's nickname from when he was in the military. "Comrade," I said, "What is going on outside, and who are all those people hanging around out front?"

My dad turned to me and said, "Cut the lights out, and let's get down on our knees and crawl over to the front door."

"What? I don't want to get on your dirty floor and crawl to the door," I said.

"Just be quiet and do it," he whispered.

I said, "It's pitch dark in here, and I can't see anything." I couldn't see that he had some firecrackers in his hand.

"Crack the front door open," he said.

"What are you going to do?" I said.

Dad said, "Watch this," and he lit and tossed several firecrackers out the door. BANG! BANG! BANG! His excitement was like a kid at Christmas. Fifteen to twenty people ran off as fast as they could while trying to figure out where all that noise came from.

My dad was on the ground laughing his heart out.

I said, "Man, you are crazy!"

My dad looked at me with a glass of gin in his hand and said, "You see that color TV sitting over there? Every house on the block has been broken into. I want to make sure they think twice about coming in here. I am not crazy, son, I just want them to think that I am."

In spite of his flaws I enjoyed spending time with my dad and learned a lot from him. He taught me about life on the streets — what it was like, how to protect myself, and to keep an eye on what's going down.

He had this saying that he repeated regularly, "Don't take any wooden nickels." This phrase was his lighthearted reminder to be cautious in my dealings, always alert, and to avoid being victimized.

Dad had no mentors, no one to lead him. He was a loner, and the environment he had created for himself was all about survival.

Through my dad, I had absorbed a lot about the streets. However, during the time spent with him it became clear to me that his lifestyle wasn't the kind I wanted. From observing him and others I was able to decide what lifestyle would work best for me in reaching my dreams. But, it remains important to me to never forget where I came from. My aim is to always stay humble and grateful for every aspect of my past.

CHOOSE MENTORS CAREFULLY AND LISTEN WELL!

CHAPTER FIVE

COLLEGE
BOUND

CHAPTER FIVE

COLLEGE BOUND

I GRADUATED FROM WOODRUFF HIGH SCHOOL IN THE SPRING OF 1977. My goal was to look for a college to further my education and extend my baseball career. My dream was to attend Arizona State University (ASU) because my favorite player and idol, Reggie Jackson, got his start playing for the Arizona State Sun Devils. It was one of the most prominent schools in the country for baseball. Quite a number of pro baseball players have been drafted out of Arizona State University.

WESTBOUND

I thought that by attending a junior college, I might get noticed by the ASU coaches and get recruited. So I attended Arizona Western Junior College. This college seemed a good fit for me.

I set out for Arizona, lonely but excited. The plane ride from Peoria to Phoenix was terrifying! It was my first time on a plane. But the worst part of the trip was from Phoenix to Yuma. It was all desert. I looked out the window and I was in a different world. There was so much sand, heat, and swirling wind.

The flight gave me some time to reflect on being on my own for the first time in my life. All I could think about was my family and friends plus the baseball coach picking me up at the airport.

I stepped off the plane and was greeted by the coach. After checking into the dormitory, we headed to the baseball diamond to field some ground balls and discuss being a walk-on without a scholarship. I had no guarantee, but the coach was willing to give me a chance when the official try-outs started.

I was homesick, especially when my grandma called me and told me to keep the doors locked. I hadn't thought about locking the doors, but I followed her direction. I missed my grandma's home-cooked meals and my family. Summer in Yuma was over one hundred degrees. My first weeks there were hot and lonely. I wasn't sure what to expect from this new school. I also didn't know what specific field I wanted to pursue.

I stayed for one semester of general education classes and felt I had made the wrong decision. Attending school out in the desert was boring with nothing to do, no friends, and no car. I needed to determine whether I would stay the duration or leave. Having no mentors to help me make decisions, I called my dad and asked him what to do. He suggested that I leave.

Dad told me to go to Los Angeles, California, and visit his brother, Joe Bowie. I made a rash decision and left Arizona, after being there for less than six months, and went to Los Angeles. Later, I found out that the San Diego Padres had a training camp in Yuma, at Arizona Western Junior College, where I had tried out for the baseball team. San Diego Padres scouts could have seen me play and recruited me. Taking advice from my dad was the wrong call.

I had dreamed my whole life for this opportunity and I made a mistake by leaving school early. I got caught up focusing on the wrong things and let negative thoughts dwell in my head. I don't blame anyone, but I literally dropped the ball.

Arizona was my legitimate shot at baseball, but I didn't realize it. I was right where I should have been. "Never make a rash decision," is what I learned from that episode. At the same time, I now know that no one can ever be guaranteed they will succeed, but when you never bet on yourself and don't try something new, you definitely guarantee that you will never succeed. To reach my dreams, I knew it was essential to be in action, even though it may not always be a straight path.

CALIFORNIA DREAMING

When the plane circled Los Angeles, I saw all the lights, which got me excited to be there. I wanted to try out for the baseball team at El Camino Junior College, but the team had been picked and had already started their season. I was too late.

I slept on my uncle Joe's couch for one year, attended school during the day, and played semi-pro baseball in the summer league. It was expensive to attend El Camino Junior College. Uncle Joe's living environment made it impossible to study. It consisted of dominoes and card games all night. After attending only two semesters, I had to part ways with sunny Southern California.

I still had baseball in the back of my mind. I had big dreams and a vision, but thought I had nothing to offer anyone at that time. I thanked my uncle for taking me in, but I had to put California on hold and rethink my plans. Sometimes in life, you have to accept wrong choices and try and do better next time.

I considered my potential career. Things would take time. I needed to change my focus and mindset. It was hard to leave California, but I did because I wanted to do something outstanding with my life. I wanted to make a name for myself.

I went back to Peoria, Illinois and attended Illinois Central College in East Peoria. My heart was set on being the first one in my family to graduate from college. I found odd jobs along the way. I worked at the car wash on Main Street, and later I became a waiter in the Raintree Restaurant at the Continental Regency Hotel in Downtown Peoria.

After attending Illinois Central College for a couple of semesters, I took a year off. I played baseball in the Sunday morning league with the Illinois Furniture team to fill the void. I got back into the swing of things and realized how much I missed baseball.

I regrouped and focused on what I really wanted to do and what was important. I felt in my spirit that I could make it in baseball. I thought, "I'll have one more run at baseball." I realized that I had also started to enjoy school and I was determined to make my mom proud by graduating.

The Illinois Furniture summer league team asked me to play shortstop and I played all season with them. The team took me in like family. I was thrilled to play and be back in the game — what a great group of players with so much talent! I was hitting the ball well and had a .364 batting average.

WESTERN ILLINOIS UNIVERSITY

The St. Louis Cardinals hosted a free tryout for local baseball players. I had nothing to lose. To get a chance to show the St. Louis Cardinals what I could do on the field would be a lifetime experience. I didn't set any expectations for myself. It would be a long shot to make the team.

The tryout consisted mainly of running and fielding. Afterward, as I walked off the field, a local scout came over and inquired about what college I'd be attending. I told him Western Illinois University (WIU), and he said he would keep an eye out for me. The Cardinals didn't sign anyone that day, but playing on that field was a special moment I will always cherish.

During the summer, I received a call from the baseball coach at WIU. He was excited that I was having a great summer playing with Illinois Furniture. I thought I could make his baseball team and that succeeding there would be a way into the big leagues. Since I was a walk-on at WIU, I had to save my money to pay for school. With the help of financial aid, I got the opportunity to attend WIU and try out for the baseball team.

I checked into my dorm room and made friends who listened to all types of music that piqued my interest. Dwayne Banks and Johnny Washington, who played basketball for WIU were two of those friends. We had a lot of fun playing cards and listening to George Benson. I enjoyed hanging out with them and took a liking to the recording artist Sting.

Baseball tryouts were based on how well you could run, hit, and field. I was clocked from home plate to first base at 3.9 seconds, and at that time Willie Wilson of the Kansas City Royals was one of the fastest in baseball at about 3.7 seconds. My batting average was over .300. Fielding was my specialty, and I took pride in getting to the ball fast. I had to race one of my teammates to make the team. I won the race, but the coach gave the position to the other player.

Things didn't work out in my favor. I was cut from the baseball team. I realized, "It's not what you know, but who you know." Most of the players were from the same small town outside of St. Louis, Missouri.

There was a player on the team who received more scholarship money than anyone else. His family members were boosters who put on bake sales that helped raise funds for the baseball team. He was a pitcher with a fastball that was clocked around seventy miles an hour, which was more like Little League. His mom must have made some really good brownies.

When I didn't see my name on the list of those chosen for the team, I was shocked. So were some of the players from the previous year. I told the coach, "You might cut me from the baseball team, but you will not keep me from my degree!"

I knew I could succeed at something. I had to believe in myself — that I would make it. I looked deep inside myself. I went for long walks thinking of all kinds of possibilities. It became clear that I liked meeting people and building relationships. I was not sure what was next for me other than this: God gives all of us more than one gift.

I could be the first in my family to graduate from college. Having a degree was very appealing to me. The void of baseball was behind me, and my positive energy was back. Getting a degree could open doors, and I would have something to offer when I went back to California.

GRADUATION

I came home from school every weekend to wait tables at the Raintree Restaurant. Waiting tables helped me to think of others and how I could be of service. It also opened my mind to dreaming big and unlimited ideas.

My manager used to have a contest every night to see which waiter could sell the most deserts. My competitive spirit came forth and I started winning. I became aware I had a gift for selling and used it. The most important aspect of selling is to start with a smile and the end will be a piece of cake. (Yes, I meant that pun.) I truly enjoyed delighting my customers.

On weekends I also wanted to spend more time with my family. Mom had a friend named Preston Jackson who went to the same church as our family, the Ward Chapel AME (African Methodist Episcopal Church). Preston played the guitar for the church. He invited me to come to one of his Tai Chi classes and we became friends. Preston saw my vision. He helped me to focus after baseball and expand my ideas about life. This was the second time in my life that I was mentored.

Preston had many gifts that inspired me. We discussed a variety of topics, from cars to music. He had a love for the "art of sculpture." He was also a professor at WIU and gave me rides to school during the last year and a half that I attended. The life of my old 1968 Impala had run its course, and I didn't want to get stranded on the highway, so Preston was a blessing and the timing was perfect.

I completed all of my general studies and decided to get a degree in communications. My customers, and others, had often told me that I was good at sales. My grade point average started to rise, and my focus was on more than baseball. I envisioned going back to California.

In the summer of 1984 I completed all the requirements for my degree from Western Illinois University.

Mom and Charles attended my graduation. I was excited about graduating. It was hard to put on my graduation cap with my big afro but I got it on and slung the tassel to the right. Then at the end of the ceremony I slung the tassel to the left. At that moment, I knew that dreams do come true. Baseball was behind me. God had other plans for my life.

BELIEVE IN YOURSELF!

CHAPTER SIX

MY FIRST PRIVATE JET RIDE

MY FIRST PRIVATE JET RIDE

I WORKED MY WAY UP TO HEADWAITER AT THE RAINTREE RESTAURANT. I took pride in serving each customer. My appearance was top-notch, and I was cordial, hospitable, observant, and attentive. Guests would stand in line and wait to get into my section. My manager trusted me to take care of the guests to the best of my ability and, at times, let me service all the tables in the restaurant. On those occasions, I told the supervisor to leave me a few busboys and someone to get drinks, and I would take care of every guest.

One night Diana Ross had a concert at the Peoria Civic Center. I heard a group of people laughing and talking as they came into the restaurant. As I looked up, I saw Diana and her entourage heading straight to my section. I was enthusiastic about serving them and about meeting Diana. She was gracious and kind to me. And it was fun to serve her.

Every time the Civic Center had an event, some of the entertainers and audience would spill over into the restaurant, and I had the privilege of serving the celebrities. I specifically recall one basketball game at the Civic Center, the Chicago Bulls vs. the Indiana Pacers. This was a preseason game and Michael Jordan's debut in the NBA. After the game, a few of the players came into the Raintree Restaurant for dinner.

On my birthday, I invited all my family members and a few neighbors to come to the restaurant to serve them dinner. What happened then was one of the most embarrassing things that ever happened to me while waiting tables. I was carrying a big tray full of food and desserts. I slipped on some butter on the floor, and the tray flew into the air. As I fell, it landed on top of my head. I was covered with whipped cream from head to toe. I didn't want to go back out in front of my family. When I finally got the courage to go back to the table, my family clapped and cheered. Talk about embarrassment!

Being of service to others opened my mind to many possibilities that would help me develop people skills. I realized that guests would rely on me to make suggestions on the menu. I became a trusted advisor.

The average time spent with guests was two hours. Body language and eye contact with the guest helped me know when to approach the table and when to stay back. The last thing I wanted to do was interrupt a guest in the middle of a business deal or a couple in a deep conversation. I was learning sales techniques that later would be pivotal in my sales career and didn't even know it. Timing is everything in life. You never know who you are going to meet, and my motto was "Treat everyone with dignity and respect and pick up a few pointers along the way."

BUILDING RELATIONSHIPS

A gentleman was sitting in my section when I came to work at the restaurant one day. I had seen him before, but didn't know him. After he had dinner, I took the check to his table and he said, "Don't bring the check to the owner of the hotel." His name was Ray Becker.

I didn't know he owned the hotel. But I made a great connection with Ray that day, and as a result I was able to help my brother Larry get a job playing the piano in the bar. I also got a job for my brother Charles as a bellhop.

Ray held business meetings at the hotel and would bring guests into the restaurant. Ray and I set up a communication method to let me know when he needed service during a meeting. I was conscious not to disturb the meetings, but when Ray tapped twice on the table, I made sure to provide excellent service to him and his guests.

I liked Ray's focus on business, and it made me dream that one day I could become a businessman too. Ray liked the fact that I had a strong passion and vision for my life. Ray and I completed a few business deals, including a family matter which helped my grandma and grandpa complete the sale of their house.

One day Ray came into the Raintree Restaurant for a business meeting and waited for me to finish waiting on other customers. He always watched me as I handled every customer's needs with grace and finesse. When I arrived at his table, he told me about a trip he was going to take. "Glenn, I'm going to San Diego, California, to a fundraiser for Betty Ford. I'm going to meet Alex Spanos, owner of the San Diego Chargers, and a few others. Would you like to serve drinks on my private jet?"

At that time, I was focused on returning to California, and now it was within reach. I tried to contain myself, to be calm before I answered, "Of course I will go to California with you. I appreciate the opportunity."

I went home excited that day and told my mom that Mr. Ray Becker had asked me to go to California and serve drinks on his private jet. I told her I was not going to return to Peoria. "Is that okay, mom?" Mom knew that I wanted to get back to California. "Son, go for it! Make your dreams come true," mom said. "Taking the trip back to California is a great opportunity for you."

That day, I made mom a promise. I said, "No matter how this all works out, I'm going to come back and get you, and you're going to come to California and live with me so I can take care of you. My word is my bond!"

I met Mr. Becker at the Twin Towers Condominiums. He had a penthouse that occupied two floors. Ray took me up on the roof and showed me the whole city of Peoria, then presented me with an offer. He said, "When you get to California, and if things don't work out, you can always come work for me."

My first private jet ride to San Diego was smooth for a while, at least while I served drinks and watched Ray and his friends play cards. Then the ride turned rough because the plane ran into a storm over the mountains of Denver, Colorado. Mr. Kennedy, the pilot, asked me to sit in the cockpit. I was the copilot in my mind, but I was scared to death. The storm went on for an hour that seemed like forever. I could not see anything but clouds, rain, and lightning.

The plane was rocked by turbulence as the pilot talked over the airways to the traffic controller. I cried out to the Lord to help me, "Lord, please forgive me for all my sins, and the pain I may have caused anyone. Please forgive the baseball coach who cut me from the team." All of a sudden, the sky opened up and the turbulence stopped. After that experience, I have always kept God first in my life.

I was so glad when the plane landed.

When the flight was over, Mr. Becker looked at me and said, "What do you want to do now?"

"I want to go to Los Angeles," I said.

Mr. Becker told me to call his bank on Monday morning. When I made the call, the teller said, "Mr. Becker would like to give you a gift of five thousand dollars."

I contacted Mr. Becker to express my appreciation and said, "I will accept that gift on one condition only, and that's if I can pay the money back." I did within six months.

My brother lived in San Diego, and I stayed with him for one month. San Diego ran at a slow pace, and I wanted to live at a faster pace. I thought, "The larger the city, the larger the opportunity." I needed to get myself to Los Angeles.

TREAT OTHERS
WITH DIGNITY
AND RESPECT.

CHAPTER SEVEN

Los Angeles
on My Mind

CHAPTER SEVEN

LOS ANGELES ON MY MIND

I HEADED NORTH ON THE 405 FREEWAY TO LOS ANGELES. I wanted to meet the highly influential and always controversial, Richard Pryor, who was an inspiration to me. I felt in my spirit that I could be a success like Richard.

When I arrived in Los Angeles, I called my cousin Joe Somerville, who worked at Warner Brothers Studios and said, "Hey, cousin Joe, this is your cousin Glenn. Is it possible that you can get me on the studio lot to see Richard Pryor? I know you work on the same studio lot."

RICHARD PRYOR

Joe was happy to help. "Sure, no problem, I'll get you past the security guard. If you see a Rolls Royce parked there, then he is around." Joe drove me past the security guard and dropped me off. I told Joe to meet me at Taco Bell across the street in about thirty minutes as I hurried off to meet Richard Pryor.

Knock, knock, knock. I stood outside Richard Pryor's office, and heard a sweet voice from the inside say, "Come in." It was Marketa Cheeks, Richard's assistant. I walked into Richard's office with my hand stretched out to shake hers and said, "I'm Glenn Bowie, a professional waiter from Peoria, Illinois. I just moved to Los Angeles, and I want to meet Mr. Richard Pryor."

"Richard is not here right now, but I will tell him you came by," Marketa replied. I showed her my driver's license to confirm who I was.

As I turned to walk away, disappointed, I heard Richard in his Mudbone voice, "Say, boy, who's your people?" He then invited me in and said, "Sit down, who is your people?"

I replied, "I'm related to the Bush family. My uncle Charles Bush told me to look you up if I ever went to California."

Richard smiled and said, "Oh, I remember that boy, he used to play the saxophone in the clubs in Peoria."

I quickly threw out names to connect with Richard, "I know the Cannon family that owned Cannon Liquors, and Bris Collins," which put a smile on Richard's face. We talked about Ray Becker and things happening in Peoria.

"Well, I'm glad you're out here now," Richard said. "So, what are you going to do?"

"I'm going to look for a job waiting tables or doing something here in Hollywood."

"Marketa, get this boy's number. I want to put him in my movie," Richard said.

"Movie?"

"Yeah, I'm working on my life story, *Jo Jo Dancer*, about Peoria," Richard explained. "We are shooting a scene, and are about done with the filming, but I am going to put you in as an extra at the end. We finish filming next week," Richard smiled, shook my hand, and said, "See you next week on the movie set."

"Can I bring someone with me?"

"Yeah, who do you want to bring?" Richard asked.

"I want to bring my sister René." I thought it would be a good idea to share the experience with her — and she could also be my witness to my family that this actually happened. Marketa took down my phone number and told me where I needed to be.

I left Richard's office motivated and anxious to get my career started in Los Angeles. "What am I going to do with my life?" I asked myself. Then I met Joe at Taco Bell for lunch.

I asked Joe if I could ride around with him as he drove to work every day. Joe had the coolest job you could imagine: dropping off scripts to movie stars' houses. It would be a fun way for me to learn my way around the city. "Can you drop me off in Burbank?" Joe agreed to help me out. He said he wished he had come along with me to meet Richard Pryor on the set, but he had to work.

René and I arrived on Richard Pryor's movie set excited about being in the audience as Richard came on the stage. The stage scene was the last scene in the movie, and we were in the audience of around 2,500 people. They were shooting him doing standup comedy in this auditorium. Then we heard someone call out, "Action! Camera! Rolling!"

We were thrilled. We couldn't believe we were watching Richard with our own eyes. He was telling jokes and sharing his story about how he came back to life after his near-death experience. We also hoped we could spend some time with him at the end of all this. Richard directed the movie and gave us a few close-up shots on the screen. I didn't realize how long it takes to shoot a scene.

As I sat in the audience I was thinking and anticipating my next career move. I felt inspired. René talked about starting her skin care business, and I said I wanted to find a job and get into sales.

René and I listened to Richard's stand-up all day and laughed for hours. When the filming ended, Richard's bodyguard took us to visit Richard in his trailer. I was very grateful that Richard took time out for us, and I was happy to share the experience with my sister. I was empowered and ready to make a name for myself.

Imagine this. We walked into the living room as Richard was sitting there with a towel around his neck from all the sweat. He asked if we wanted to eat some ice cream. I was starving and jumped at the idea.

We ended up eating Dove bars and talking to Richard for twenty minutes, then parted ways.

I left there knowing that "the sky's the limit" and with determination to "make my dreams come true."

A TASTE OF HOLLYWOOD

I enjoyed the media and entertainment environment. Cousin Joe dropped me off in Hollywood the next day, as I began a daily routine of hunting for a job, wearing the same suit day after day. That lasted a while as I distributed five to ten resumes per day to entertainment-related businesses and studios. Determination and perseverance would make the difference.

I interviewed at Dick Clark Productions and at photo and printing companies. WEA (Warner-Elektra-Atlantic) Records called me for a job, but they could not get in contact with me, so I lost the job offer. (There were no cell phones back in those days.) After that I wondered what my life would have been like, working in the record industry, but I also had to tell myself that it wasn't meant to be.

Thirty days passed, and I had gotten frustrated. It seemed that everywhere I went, someone would tell me, "You need to get two years of sales experience, then we will hire you." I heard that over and over again, even in my sleep. I tried to hire on at Universal Studios, and at Walt Disney in the mail room, but I genuinely wanted to get into sales.

Having a college degree does not guarantee you a job, but persistence does. The more potential job opportunities that turned me down, the more doors I knocked on. My motto was "Never give up. Never give in. Just believe you *can* make it!"

One day, at the end of a long job hunt, I looked up and saw this massive glass building at Universal Studios sitting on a hill. It was the Sheraton Premiere Hotel, and it was calling my name. I told my cousin Joe to drop me off there.

As I got out of his truck, I saw a man walking out of the hotel. I walked up to him, shook his hand and said, "Sir, my name is Glenn Bowie, I'm a professional waiter from Peoria, Illinois, and I want to wait tables in this hotel."

I had put a strategy together. I figured someone would hire me if I could be of service to someone else. I decided to go with what I knew from my college days which was waiting tables. By waiting tables I believed I could build relationships and get connections that would eventually lead to a sales job.

The man looked at me and smiled. He was Herb Hunter, the Director of Guest Services. "We don't have any waiter positions open, but I would like to hire you as a bellhop," he said.

I kept the faith that God uses people to help you.

"Great! When can I start?" I went through two interviews, and that's when I knew that I needed to put on my sales hat. My third interview was with Herb's boss who asked, "Why would you want to be a bellhop? You have a four-year degree." All the previous job interviews had prepared me for this day.

I replied, "I have to start somewhere. I have to get an apartment, establish credit, and get a car. Please give me a chance. I promise you, I will be the best bellhop you have ever had, and I will stay here for a minimum of five years." She looked me straight in the eye and said, "You've got the job!"

I started a week later and only then found out that this was the hotel for movie stars. It was a partnership of Universal Studios, MCA Records and Sheraton.

I had to wear a uniform and take the bus from Inglewood to Universal City daily. It was a three-hour bus ride back and forth that traveled through some dangerous parts of Los Angeles. I couldn't wait to save my money and one day get a car and an apartment in Studio City, ten minutes from work. Having a uniform and locker at work allowed me to dress down to fit in with the crowd as a means of survival when I rode that graveyard-shift bus. It kept me humble.

Being on the graveyard shift was my entry-level position. I had to work my way up to day shift, but I didn't mind. It became a pleasant surprise when I found out that all the action in that hotel happened after midnight.

GRAVEYARD SHIFT

My first day on the job, I checked Paul Winfield into his King's Corner room on the 24th floor, around the corner from the Presidential Suite, which went for twenty-four hundred a night.

The hotel named the room King's Corner because it had spectacular views and the rooms were bigger and highly sought after. You were given a choice of views: downtown Los Angeles, Hollywood Hills or San Fernando Valley, which was my favorite as it overlooked Universal Studios and Lakeside Golf Course. Paul Winfield, who played Martin Luther King, Jr. in the three-part TV Series "King: The Martin Luther King Jr. Story," gave me my first tip.

My first tip felt good, but in the back of my mind I could hear my mom saying, "Don't take any money from people." I felt bad about it, but after a few weeks I realized that it was a part of my job to service the guests and receive tips.

Every day I looked at the printout of what movie stars would be coming to the hotel. If you were a movie star or a recording artist, you stayed at the Sheraton Premiere Hotel. My job was so much fun that it was not even work for me. It was like going to a party every night.

I met everyone from the Pope to the President. I met Walter Payton of the Chicago Bears and we became close friends shortly after they won the Super Bowl. Walter invited me to come to Chicago to visit next time I was in Peoria.

When I was home visiting mom for Thanksgiving she encouraged me to give Walter a call. Walter invited me to hang out in Chicago. I went to Studebaker's Restaurant owned by Walter, and we listened to music in his office. We talked about sports and business ideas and had a great time.

He was showing his appreciation for my hospitality back in Los Angeles, when I had picked him up at the airport in a vintage Rolls Royce and showed him some great restaurants in Hollywood.

Walter took me under his wing and I became known as Little Glenn, because he had a friend named Big Glenn. We had a lot of good times over the years.

My favorite visit with him was the following summer, when I went to the Long Beach Grand Prix celebrity race to watch Walter drive his car. At that race he had his own racing team, with his trailer located down in the pit. I had great fun hanging out down there with his team, and the grill kept everyone well fed through the excitement of race day.

Today Walter Payton is in the Pro Football Hall of Fame. The NFL gives out a trophy in his name every year. My own "trophy" is a Wheaties box that he autographed for me. My friends cherish the signed footballs he provided me to give to them.

NOTHING HAPPENS IN LIFE UNTIL YOU STEP OUT OF YOUR COMFORT ZONE.

CHAPTER EIGHT

BELLHOP
TO THE STARS

BELLHOP TO THE STARS

FOR SIX MONTHS, I LIVED WITH MY SISTER RENÉ IN INGLEWOOD, CA. I was very grateful to her for letting me stay with her, and I enjoyed driving with René to the nearby Los Angeles International Airport to watch the airplanes land. It inspired me to reach a higher level in life and encouraged me to dream big.

Transportation was a problem for me until Beverly, a sister of Herb Hunter, sold me her Honda Civic.

Then I moved to Studio Colony in Studio City just ten minutes away from Hollywood. My neighbors were a variety of movie stars: Alyssa Milano of "Who's the Boss," Bret Michaels the lead singer of the band Poison, Dawnn Lewis of "A Different World," and the Butler from the "Fresh Prince of Bel-Air" — to name just a few.

My apartment had one big room, a closet, and a bathroom. I was so proud and thankful that it was brand new. I did not care that it was small. I didn't have much in it at first, and the hotel provided uniforms, so I didn't have to spend much on clothes. I stayed in Studio City for a long time.

The hotel was exciting, nonstop. The Black Radio Exclusive convention was held at the hotel every year. It was the place to be, and the most popular thing to do. Every record company had a suite in the hotel.

Prince held a concert there along with Klymaxx. I became friends with the lead singer of Klymaxx, Bernadette Cooper, who also had a limousine service called Cooper's Limousine. I sent Bernadette so much business that she hired me to drive the band to concerts and shows. I drove everywhere, using my Thomas Guide and magnifying glass. After a year, I decided I was spending too much time doing it, and I needed my rest.

I built a good relationship with the hotel manager, who gave me the hotel's vintage Rolls Royce at my discretion to promote the hotel and take celebrities out on the town. Monier, the hotel driver, and I would stock the car with champagne and strawberries and hit the town. We would split tips every night.

Everyone in my neighborhood thought I was a celebrity because I had my own driver pick me up in a vintage Rolls Royce. We went to night clubs and great restaurants like Carlos 'n Charlie's and Spago.

One night I took Walter Payton to Carlos 'n Charlie's and saw Evander Holyfield. We went to his table, greeted him, and shook hands with him before going to our table. When we left I drove Walter around and took him up to Mulholland Drive. I wanted to take the scenic route so Walter could enjoy the ride. I started zigzaging through the very winding road and it made Walter feel lightheaded, so I didn't do that again.

FUN TIMES

At the hotel I never knew who I was going to meet next. It was a great experience getting to know Hollywood, but it was not always perfect — only about 99% of the time.

One day when I came to work, Oprah Winfrey was in town filming "The Women of Brewster Place," the classic story of faith and courage. I helped her get her bags up to her room. She had six vans full of clothes. Stedman was there in the room as I came and went, bringing up more clothes and Oprah's packages. Oprah had just launched her show. She gave me an Oprah shirt, which I sent home to mom. Oprah made sure we were all taken care of, and we wanted to make her stay special.

One Friday night, I was excited about meeting my friends to go out and dance, but my manager asked me to stay overtime and wait for the arrival of Michael Jackson. Sitting in the back talking with the switchboard operator around 2:30 A.M., the hotel was empty, and there were no reservations.

I came out from the back with my head down, but I saw someone standing over in the corner when I looked up. As I got closer, I saw a man with a Dodgers baseball cap. He wore a Lakers jacket, blue jeans, Air Jordans, and a surgical mask over his face. Must be Michael Jackson, I thought. I walked up to him and introduced myself, "Mr. Jackson, my name is Glenn Bowie, I am a professional bellhop from Peoria, Illinois, and I'm here to take care of you. I'm going to hide you from the paparazzi and make sure no one bothers you. I'm going to make your stay an enjoyable one."

In his very distinct voice, Michael said, "Thank you!"

After a few days of helping Michael's private chef bring his specially prepared food up to his room, I asked her, "Does Michael ever come out of his room?" She said, "Just look for the old man with a cane."

While I was standing at the bellhop desk by the front door I saw an older man walking down the corridor with a cane. "Must be Michael," I thought. He walked up and stood right beside me. He winked at me to confirm his identity, and I winked back. People came in and out of the hotel, asking me if I had seen Michael Jackson because they knew he was in the hotel somewhere. "No, I have not seen him," I replied, with Michael standing right next to me.

Michael was working on his *BAD* album. He stayed in the Presidential Suite for a couple of months. One day when I was standing out in front of the hotel, I saw Michael's limousine come around the corner. I wondered why he had come out that way. Michael rolled down the window and started screaming, "Glenn! Glenn! Glenn! I lost my key! What am I going to do? Come! Come!" I ran to his limousine. Michael opened up the door and I jumped in. The paparazzi chased the car down the street yelling, "There's Michael!" and "He's here! He's here!"

Michael was laughing his head off. I used his car phone to call Security. I explained that the paparazzi were chasing Michael, and I was going to go with him up to Universal Studios and back to get away from them. Security should meet us at the loading dock. We finally ditched the paparazzi, and I got Michael back to his room.

As time went on, I met many more celebrities. At one point Steve Perry, the lead singer for the band Journey, was staying at the hotel. The band had just broken up, and Steve was trying to figure out what he was going to do next.

I never bothered celebrities. They respond like ordinary people. If you leave them alone, they get curious to find out who you are. If you want to get to know them, doing the exact opposite of what they are used to works. So I gave Steve his space.

One day he pulled up in his Corvette. I stood in a corner, and Steve came over to me and said, "I like how you respect my privacy." The other bellhops wondered why Steve took a liking to me. "You never ask me for anything," Steve said.

"I know the other bellhops always ask you for autographs," I said.

Steve said, "Do you want an autograph to give to someone?"

"How about for Debbie, my next-door neighbor. She loves you," I said.

Steve asked me to help him up to his room and carry his packages. He also asked me to listen to some of his new music. It was soulful music, and it sounded smooth like Marvin Gaye. I gave Steve the thumbs-up. When I got back to my apartment, I found out that Debbie had moved, so I ended up with Steve's autograph after all.

Marcus Miller, a famous bass player nicknamed "Juice," arrived at the hotel one night. When I told him I was one of his biggest fans since high school and still owned his first solo album, he was pleased. As we arrived in his room with the luggage, he asked if I wanted to listen to a song he had just recorded with David Sanborn. After listening to the song, I asked, "What are you going to name it?"

"I'm not sure," said Marcus. "Where are you from?"

"I'm from Peoria, Illinois, about a couple of hours southwest of Chicago." He ended up naming it "Chicago Song." To this day, I wonder if our encounter inspired his decision.

I would never have known who Marcus was if it hadn't been for Peoria's own Lloyd Henderson. Lloyd was a music connoisseur. He introduced me to a lot of music and musicians, including the artist Narada Michael Walden, who wrote some hit songs for Aretha Franklin and Whitney Houston.

One day I looked at the hotel reservation sheet and Narada Michael Walden's name was on it. I thought, "Man, how cool is this, I'm going to get a chance to meet Narada!" That was a special moment. Narada's music touched my heart and soul. As I helped him to his room, I shared what each of his albums had meant to me. He was impressed that I was so knowledgeable about all of his lyrics and music.

It was like a party every day at the Sheraton Premiere Hotel. You never knew who you were going to meet: Frank Sinatra,

Tom Hanks, Denzel Washington, Andre Harrell, Rob Lowe, the Isley Brothers, Patti LaBelle, Gladys Knight, to name a few. I kept a diary during those years and that could be another book all by itself.

I would sneak VIPs upstairs through the kitchen, and up the service elevator. But I told everyone that I didn't do drugs. I didn't do anything illegal or not approved by the hotel.

All these memories are etched in my mind. I had a lot of fun times every day. But those years, most importantly, taught me about giving without expecting anything in return.

Most celebrities were extremely nice. Some stars were arrogant and not friendly at all. I had to learn how to read people to know if they were friendly or not. I thought about what my mom always told me, "Treat everyone with respect."

MUHAMMAD ALI – THE CHAMP

It was an extraordinary moment when I met Muhammad Ali. I checked him in along with his wife, and Muhammad gave me a fifty-dollar tip for two pieces of luggage.

On many occasions, I would reserve a room for my brother Charles at the hotel to share the experience with him. So I got on the phone and called my brother in San Diego and invited him to the hotel to meet Muhammad.

One day I took Muhammad his mail and his photographer was in the room. Muhammad asked me to shadowbox with him. He said, "Put your hand on my cheek." I put my dukes up although nervous because I didn't want to make Muhammad flashback thinking he was back in the ring and get walloped! But I received a great treasure that day — a photo of Muhammad and me shadowboxing in his room.

He was tremendously nice, caring, and good-spirited. He would always ask me if I was by myself in case he needed to tip someone else besides me. He took a genuine liking to me and would call down to the bellhop desk and ask for me if he needed anything.

At one Black Radio Exclusive (BRE) convention I met Patti LaBelle's writers and producers, and Sami McKinney, a big-time writer whom I met through Bernadette Cooper. He was a songwriter for Anita Baker, Nancy Wilson, and George Duke.

The annual BRE convention eventually got out of control because too many people came once it was announced on the radio. And so many entertainers were having such a great time in the suites that the police had to be on-site. They even threatened to shut the place down. There were cars backed up all the way down the 101 Freeway from the hotel to downtown L.A. Finally the hotel stopped holding the event because the large crowds were unsafe.

My advice to those who are shy is to get themselves into the service industry. You can learn communication skills, people skills, and build good relationships.

I started as a waiter and ended up a bellhop to the stars. My biggest takeaway is that people are just people and it's best to show respect and treat everyone the same regardless of race, ethnicity or social background. Today, at least once a month I drive through Skid Row to remind myself how blessed I am.

As entertaining as it was being a bellhop to the stars, I knew in the back of my mind that one day mom was going to need me and I wanted to prepare myself for that day. I had outgrown the hotel. I had kept my five-year commitment and was ready to make a difference in the world. But I was not sure of the path to take.

I had my degree in my pocket with the thought of getting into sales. However I still didn't have the experience. I prayed that someone would give me an opportunity in sales.

I wanted to make something of myself. I would work hard and make a corporation very proud to have me on their team. I had to step out on faith. Hmmm... I considered the possibilities. My experience in the hotel business had prepared me for my next adventure.

DREAMS DO COME TRUE. KEEP ON, KEEPING ON!

CHAPTER NINE

THE ART
OF A SALESMAN

THE ART
OF A SALESMAN

AFTER A FEW MONTHS MY FRIEND HERB HUNTER, WHO HAD HIRED ME at the Sheraton Premiere Hotel, came back to visit me there. Herb had moved on and was now working for PageNet (also known as Paging Network Inc.). Herb said, "Glenn, I know you have always wanted to get into sales, and I'm going to give you your first shot."

BEFORE THERE WERE CELL PHONES

Before there were cell phones, there were pagers. Herb told me about the opportunities in that field. After talking with him, I was looking forward to getting my feet wet in the paging industry. I was burnt-out after being in the hotel industry for five years.

Herb hired me as an Account Executive for PageNet. He said, "Let's see what you can do!" I was given a huge territory that included all of Los Angeles — down to Manhattan Beach and over to East Los Angeles.

On my first day out in the field, Herb explained the function of a pager and the target market. "This is a new way of communication," he said. Then he told me the accounts I would be covering: 20th Century Fox, CBS, Culver Studios, MGM, Xerox, Hughes Aircraft, and other major corporations. "That should keep you busy!"

The bulk of my business came out of 20th Century Fox Studios. I had never been on a studio lot before, except when I met Richard Pryor at Warner Brothers Studios. It was pretty fascinating. The TV shows "Doogie Howser, M.D." and "L.A. Law" with Blair Underwood, and the movie *The War of the Roses* with Michael Douglas were a few of my clients. I was on the lot at least once a day dropping off pagers to the production crews.

I decided to watch a couple of takes of Blair Underwood performing his role, and it was fascinating to see him in character. In between signing up clients for pagers, I watched them film for a few minutes and thought about all the long hours it takes to make a TV show. But I was inspired by it. And who would have thought that Blair and I would become good friends a few years later?

I was enthused about visiting all of the production companies in the area. It was a fast-paced industry and I was selling pagers fast. I stocked the pagers in the back of my 1979 Honda Civic hatchback, selling them to anybody and everybody.

This was my first taste of sales, and I was on a mission. My strategy was to see how many appointments I could get each day as I learned to sell. "Make it into a game" was my motto. I planned my days and nights and even worked on weekends while most sales representatives took off nights and weekends.

The time I spent riding around L.A. with my cousin Joe really paid off because I knew my way around the city and all the shortcuts and landmarks.

I purchased a book on sales by top sales guru Tom Hopkins called *How to Master the Art of Selling.* It taught me about building relationships, making a sale, closing a deal, looking for buyers, establishing trust, honesty, and how well you could service the account after selling. I patterned myself after Tom by following his techniques.

The type of car you drive in Los Angeles, for the kind of industry you are in, can surely make or break a deal. I didn't have to worry about that because I was selling pagers and driving a Honda. I was thinking more about saving on gas and felt blessed to have a car at all. But it was essential to understand the relationship between my vehicle and my image so I could use it to my advantage. Driving a practical vehicle helped me to find some common ground with potential clients.

I wanted the focus to be on the product not my car. So I would let the client know I was on the same level as they were, and that would make them want to buy more pagers. Some clients thought I was making a lot of money selling so they would say, "Let me see what kind of car you are driving." I had clients walk me to my car after listening to my sales pitch, see the old Honda, and realize that they weren't paying for my car. I thought to myself, "One day, when I get a new vehicle, I'll have to park blocks away!"

I shared my technique with a colleague that drove his Mercedes 500 SEL to work every day. He had struggled with sales for a year because he parked his big Mercedes right next to the small business owner's car. "Here's a tip," I said. "Do me a favor, try something for thirty days, and see if it makes a difference. You are driving a car that's nicer than the small business owner's car. So try parking your car around the corner." Sure enough, it worked. His sales started growing. He gained confidence and realized I was on to something. I told him, "You don't want the focus to be on the car. Let them focus on the product."

Once I went on an appointment with a coworker and his

cologne was so strong you could smell it before he got out of the car. It was a distraction, and the client cut the meeting short. The guy could have been allergic to it. It's the little things that make a difference.

I recall another time I went out on a cold call with a specific sales representative. The client said, "Yes, I'm ready to move forward with your product." The sales representative started upselling her right there in front of me on a different product. Under the table I gently kicked her to let her know to get the business first! She ended up not getting any sale at all.

Later the client called me and wanted to do business with me. I signed the deal for the sales representative and gave her the commission. I then pulled her aside and gave her some tips on how important it is to be a good listener, to listen twice as much as you speak. It went in one ear and out the other!

I enjoyed selling pagers, meeting people from all walks of life, and making a difference for them. It was a high-pressure job, especially when I met people who needed pagers on the spot and could not wait a day or two.

Those people would go to another competitor unless I had what they wanted on hand. The faster I could get the product to the customer, the better off I was.

I began to set a personal goal of selling ten pagers per day, five days a week, totaling fifty pagers a week for a total of two hundred pagers a month. That number was four times my sales quota.

I wanted to be a top salesman and slowly sneak up on the people that were on top of the leader board. I eventually was selling over three hundred pagers a month. I started to get recognized. I received awards for my sales ability and gained more confidence.

I challenged myself and made it a game by timing how long it took between the moment I went in for a sale, and the time I left the business with the sale. Time was money in my eyes, and speed was important to make my sales quota.

Relationship-building based on trust that I could quickly get the product to my clients was my strength. I continued to focus on it.

I added to the game by looking for a referral as my reward from the client which would lead me to even greater success. The biggest compliment a client could give me was a referral which helped me get more business.

Being a success at sales, my lifestyle started to change. I bought Italian suits and ties, and high-end shoes. I was introduced to more and more celebrities and corporate executives. I was invited to fancy restaurants to eat, so I had to look the part even if I only had a dollar in my pocket. "You never get a second chance to make a first impression."

THE POWER OF NETWORKING

At these fancy gatherings, I would sit and listen to everyone talk. It was my way of learning and understanding different personality types. Meanwhile, my taste buds changed their tune from hamburgers to salmon which started during my first trip to Vancouver, Canada. My mind was wide open, but I could hear my grandma telling me, "Stay humble! Never forget where you came from, and give God the glory."

I built trust with the security guards on the studio lots. That's when I saw the power of networking, and it made my life so much easier. I didn't mind working harder, but I also saw the value of working smarter. I called it the spider-web approach. When I could go in and get a sale and a referral to another, my web began growing.

Now, being in Los Angeles, I got the chance to do remarkable things. For example, I would go backstage and watch the filming of movies or TV shows. I thought I could become an actor for a hot minute until I went on an audition and decided acting was not for me.

I have great respect for actors who can play different characters. But selling was in my heart and soul. And I was succeeding. When one show ended, the same production manager would call me for pagers for the next show.

At the end of each year, my goals and dreams in the sales arena had come true. I became the top salesman in the paging industry for PageNet five years in a row. I had only missed my quota one time, and that one time was when I went home to see my mom during the holidays.

I could not have made this career in sales if it hadn't been for Herb Hunter, who hired and mentored me. I also had an excellent support team.

I liked the freedom and flexibility that came with making your goal every month, and I enjoyed being able to be out on the streets of Los Angeles on my own time. After driving around in Beverly Hills and looking at all the beautiful homes, I would always make it a point to drive past less desirable areas at the end of the day to remind myself how God had blessed me and to give thanks. It kept me grounded, humble, and thinking of others.

I was making a difference in the business world, but I also wanted to leave a legacy for the next generation.

At the end of every year, the company gave out an award

voucher for ten thousand dollars to be used on a trip anywhere in the world. The first time I won it, I jumped on a plane and flew home to Peoria, packed mom's bags, and took her to "paradise" with me — Maui.

Aloha! My mother had the time of her life. It was priceless to see her face when she put her feet in the Pacific Ocean for the first time. Because she has suffered from lupus all her life, and the sun's rays aggravated her condition, I carried an open umbrella as we walked on the beach.

It almost felt like we were royalty, walking the beach in 90-degree weather in this odd way. I could see how others must see us — a guy holding an umbrella for a little lady. "Must be someone significant," they would think. And they were right.

KEEP THE FAITH

Being a creature of habit, I continued to choose to go to Maui each year, my favorite island in Hawaii. I got to know the locals and all the good restaurants. And I was introduced to many delicious exotic foods.

One time in Maui, I went snorkeling by myself and was observing all the beautifully colored island fish and lost track of time. The afternoon passed, and the tide had taken me about a mile from shore. I was scared. I got light-headed and freaked out for a second. I wasn't a good swimmer. I had to get back to the beach. I said a quick prayer to God, and I heard a voice in my head say, "Turn over and flip on your back."

As I looked up at the sky, I felt the Holy Spirit was guiding me back. I watched the clouds, tried to keep calm, and started kicking. It seemed like it was taking forever. I was afraid to look over my shoulder. I concentrated on breathing until suddenly I ran out of air.

Right when I thought my life was over, I felt the sand in my hair, and I was able to stand up. I stood and shouted, "Thank you Jesus!" I dropped on the beach sand, completely exhausted, and counted my blessings. Never give up on life.

As I flew back to Los Angeles, I had plenty of time to reflect on my vacation. I thought about how short life can be and never to take life for granted. I contemplated how I could make a difference in the world: "There is more to life than meeting celebrities and corporate executives, but also timing is everything. If I could become a top sales executive, it would give me some credibility and something to hang my hat on. I could also teach others how I achieved success."

It was time to get back to selling so I could win another trip to Maui. I began working on Saturdays selling pagers at Judy's Casting in Hollywood. Judy made it mandatory for all potential actors aspiring to get into the Hollywood movie industry to have a pager. Several of today's Hollywood stars got their pagers from Judy's Casting.

I knew my way around the city and was learning more all the time. I went to any length to get the customers what they needed, no matter where they lived. I had great fun sightseeing around town while I was at it.

I read Steven Covey's books and discovered new and different sales techniques. I also listened to Les Brown and Zig Ziglar to get inspired and receive more sales techniques. They helped me to think big. I certainly already had plenty of motivation. But I wanted to get to the next level of getting people happily involved, and I needed a new challenge.

I went for a walk one night along the beach in Malibu, pondering what was in store next for my life. It was a beautiful evening. I looked up at the stars and could see their reflection on the ocean waters. I thought about how PageNet had been my first sales job. I was thankful for the opportunity it had given me to make a difference in other businesses. I'd had a great run at PageNet but there was nothing left for me to prove.

I heard the waves crashing into the rocks as I looked up at the moon. I thought, "There must be something bigger in store for me."

LEARN,
LEARN, LEARN!

CHAPTER TEN

MOVING ON UP

CHAPTER TEN

MOVING
ON UP

T HE PAGING INDUSTRY WAS DYING, AND NEW
TECHNOLOGY WAS TAKING OVER. Herb
Hunter and a few top executives moved over to Nextel
Communications, Inc. I was like gum on Herb Hunter's
shoe. He could not get rid of me.

Nor did he want to. I had proven to Herb that I could
sell and build relationships and consistently make my
quota — but most important, delight my customers.
Nextel made me an offer I could not refuse. I went right
along with Herb to be a part of his new sales team, but
I didn't know what to expect. Herb said, "It's going to
change the world."

The first day on the job, I had to do a mock presentation
on Nextel products. Top executives introduced me to the
product that I was supposed to sell. It was a big bulky
two-way radio, cell phone, messaging and pager—all in one.
It sold for over one thousand dollars.

"How am I going to sell this big bulky product?" My vision was to grow the business by going back to my old customers to get my feet wet. They would forgive me if I made any mistakes through the sale process since trust had already been established.

The next step at Nextel that day was to train for the new product and meet all my fellow team members. I was looking forward to learning how to position the product and offering a solution that would fit the customer's needs.

The training session turned out to be very informative and interactive until the trainer directed a question to me and asked, "Why would a business buy a two-way radio for over two thousand dollars?"

I replied that first and foremost people buy from people they trust, and if you gained their trust and they liked you, they would buy from you. The trainer's reply was, "There's no way any customer would ever spend that type of money because they trust and like you."

My mouth dropped to the floor. I was embarrassed and humbled at the same time. I thought to myself, "That's how I built my business at PageNet, and I was very successful doing it that way." It put some doubt in my mind for a few minutes.

NUMBERS GAME

I knew that at the end of the day, I would exceed my quota by building relationships. Sales is a numbers game, but speaking a result into existence is what I tell myself. I turned that negative comment from the trainer to a positive and used it as fuel to light a fire under me. I was focused on proving her wrong. I pumped myself up and went into action.

In the first two months, I struggled to sell two-way radios, but sales increased with time. I was focused and determined to make it. I began to sell to security companies, blue-collar workers, and manufacturing industries needing the product. By the third quarter of my first year on the job, I received my first award for outstanding sales achievement. (At this writing I have earned over 200 awards for sales excellence.)

It felt good to get recognized. I continued building my self-confidence and thinking powerful thoughts with the goal of winning more awards. I read quotes that inspired me. I upgraded my training by reading books from various motivational authors and figuring out how to get to the next level.

After a while, those big bulky phones started selling like hotcakes. I would attend Hollywood parties with that two-way radio and because people thought I was security, I didn't have to wait in the long line to get in. I would get into clubs free to pass out my cards. I got to know the limo drivers, catering companies, moving companies, and various other businesses to sell the product. I had to work overtime to make the sales.

"Referrals" are an important part of the game, and I was on a mission to make them happen. I had a back-to-the-basics approach to selling, and I wanted to reach the blue-collar workers. It was time to take the jacket off and roll up my sleeves. I put a strategy together on how I was going to reach my goal.

DETERMINATION

I had a passion for my work. I was determined to be the best that I could be. I wasn't in competition with my peers in my eyes, although that's how the company used sales games to motivate the team. My focus was to excel by working harder *and* smarter to exceed company goals.

I used some of the sales techniques that I learned from Tom Hopkins' book, but I made them my own. I created daily goals, then weekly, monthly, and yearly goals. For motivation I would treat myself to a steak dinner or purchase a new tie every time I made quota. And at the end of the year the big prize was buying a new suit.

Consistency was important to me. That was my business model. As time went on, I received awards for top salesman. I won my first President's Council award — a trip to Cabo San Lucas.

The first thing I did was jump on a plane and head to Peoria to surprise mom and get her to join me. Unfortunately, her lupus flared up and kept her from traveling, so she could not attend. I was going to stay home with mom and cancel my trip, but she insisted that I make the flight to Mexico.

Cabo San Lucas is a beautiful place. I golfed, and enjoyed what the resort had to offer, but I couldn't help thinking about mom's health. She was going to need me one day, and I needed to be able to help her. After a week in Cabo, it was time to get back to work.

THINKING OUTSIDE THE BOX

The product I was selling was getting smaller in size. I needed to focus on a new market. I thought the produce industry would be a good start. I knew I could become an industry expert in time while staying focused on solutions and customer service. The product was well-received, and volume was picking up. I liked the idea that Nextel had the best customer service in the industry, and my support team was second to none. And I had fun. Whenever I trained customers on our new products, I brought coffee and donuts.

I began to get referrals, and in my second year of selling, I won my second President's Council award — a trip to Montego Bay, Jamaica.

The hospitality was incredible. I had a golf caddy for the first time and learned to trust him to pick out the correct club for each distance. I enjoyed details he shared about the golf course and the history lesson he gave me about Jamaica.

The next day I headed to Dunn's River Falls and Park, a famous waterfall and major tourist attraction near Ocho Rios, Jamaica with a group of Nextel employees. By the time we were done I had worked up an appetite and was ready to devour some amazing jerk chicken. Jamaica motivated me. "Ya Mon!" It was time to get back to work.

Char Webster, Nextel Senior Marketing Manager, presented all kinds of incentives for customers: buy one, get one free, buy two and you can get four. The company offered sales rewards like ski trips to Big Bear, a trip to Palm Springs, and various other rewards if you were over your quota.

Palm Springs was incredible! Spa, golf, and all the great food you could eat. I fell in love with it. I was in Palm Springs for the weekend and watched Reggie Jackson, my baseball idol as a kid, in spring training. The next day my cousin Joe and I watched Marvin Hagler train at the local boxing gym, which was open to the public before his fight against Sugar Ray Leonard.

The following day I met up with John Combs, President of Nextel Communications Southwest Area, and we decided to go for a run in Joshua Tree National Park outside of Palm Springs. I thought it would be a light jog, but John was a *runner*, not a jogger. He pushed me to my limit, and then he let me win the race. John knew how to get the most out of his people, but my side ached for the rest of the afternoon.

TIMING IS EVERYTHING

John had an open-door policy. I would stop in at his office from time to time. But my motto was "If you are in the office, you are not making sales." The more I presented in front of customers, the better my chances for sales — not only for repeat business but also to find out who they did business with so I could get referrals.

I heard over and over from customers that they liked the fact that I always answered my phone. Something so simple can often lead to something big. I was alone in the office one day. As I walked by the elevator on my way to lunch my phone was ringing. I decided to answer it, "Thanks for calling Nextel, this is Glenn Bowie. May I help you?" It was Stacey Augmon, a pro basketball player for the Portland Trailblazers. He asked me to come to his house in Pasadena, California, to show him the latest phone. I was living in Studio City at the time, but had always kept Pasadena on my vision board, even as a kid. The inspiration of the mountains moved my soul.

After I presented the product to Stacey, I lingered and spent more time talking with him about the area. I asked if he knew of any new housing developments, knowing that part of speaking into existence requires sharing your dream with others. He said, "Go down the street, make a left turn, and keep going." I thanked him and took the route he described, excited to see what was in store. As I approached the community, a security guard walked out to greet me. "Paul Devon?" I said.

He looked right in my face and called me by my nickname, "Cool Papa." I hadn't seen Paul since we worked together at the Sheraton Premiere Hotel more than ten years earlier. Paul was the doorman back then, and I was the bellhop. "What are you doing here?" Paul said. "I'm looking to buy my first property," I replied. I knew immediately that this was where I wanted my new home. Mom was the motivation since I had a vision of taking care of her one day, and I needed a place where she would feel comfortable and safe.

But things did not happen fast.

I listed my top ten requirements for the perfect home, and I wasn't going to settle, no matter what! I looked at over twenty properties with realtors. I knew to keep my focus on the dream. I even lost a few realtors along the way, who thought my requirements were way too picky.

I told one realtor that I knew exactly what I was looking for, but she could not find the right fit for me, so she gave up. I promised her: "When I find my dream home, I will call you and give you the commission for all the properties you showed me." She had a look on her face that said, "Yeah, right!"

I returned to the neighborhood Stacy had shown me, but all the lots were sold. I was disappointed, but I told the complex manager, Linda, to keep my phone number, and I would visit her a few times a month.

After two years of going back and forth to visit the area and keeping a positive attitude, I received a call from Linda. She said, "We have a property that has been in litigation for the past few years. It's available, and it meets your top ten requirements." That was music to my ears. After viewing it I fell to my knees and thanked God for the blessing. I signed the papers on my birthday and gave the commission to my original realtor.

I had completed another one of my vision board goals. All my planning and hard work had paid off and I was moving on up!

PUT A PLAN TOGETHER TO HELP YOU REACH YOUR GOALS.

CHAPTER ELEVEN

CHALLENGE ACCEPTED

CHALLENGE ACCEPTED

I HAVE NOTHING BUT LOVE AND RESPECT FOR JOHN COMBS who was the President of Nextel Communications Southwest Area. He was a father figure to me and truly cared about my family which meant a lot to me. He cared about all of his staff and sales teams. As a result, we all wanted to go above and beyond to make a difference for Nextel's customers. He motivated me to reach beyond my limit.

MASTER MOTIVATOR

John challenged me to win the President's Council Award three times in a row. He asked me, "What do you want as a reward?" I said, "To have my mother flown out to Los Angeles to visit me." We shook hands in his office, and one year later I won the challenge because I had won the President's Council Award again.

True to his word, John rewarded me for winning the challenge, and rolled out the red carpet for mom and my brother, Larry, with an all-expense-paid trip to visit me. It included a trip to Las Vegas, San Diego, and of course, back to Maui. It was first class all the way. John even provided a limo driver for the two weeks mom was here in Los Angeles. It was priceless to see the smile on her face.

After winning that third President's Council Award, I was awarded a trip to Cancun, Mexico. This was in addition to winning the challenge reward from John Combs.

I packed my bags for Cancun, Mexico. Upon arrival, I spent most of my time sitting quietly out on the balcony overlooking the beautiful blue waters of the Caribbean Sea with my brother Charles. It was special to have my brother on this trip so we could spend some quality time together and bond.

I stopped by John's office upon my return to thank him for everything. I was motivated! I was ready for another run at winning the President's Council Award to keep my streak going.

PICK UP THE PHONE

The phone rang as I was leaving for a meeting one day. The receptionist was out of the office, so I picked up the phone. It was an irate customer who needed help using a

Nextel product. He was furious that no one had answered the phone, and he could not get anyone to come to his office. I said, "Give me your address and phone number, and I will drop by to help you."

When I arrived, he took me directly to his office and told me how unhappy he was about the product. I let him vent his anger and frustration. And in the end he wanted to make a purchase. He let me know that he was a Nextel investor and was friends with Bill Gates. He thanked me for coming out to help him. We exchanged business cards. I said I would take his comments back to management to see what changes needed to be made.

By doing right by this customer, he became a referral source which helped me gain more customers in his field. He also became a friend and a mentor who helped me continue to dream big. We talked about goal setting, planning for the future, and always answering your phone — which I did.

It turned out that the switchboard operator had done me a big favor that day by taking lunch without rolling the phones over to voicemail.

The Nextel i1000 Plus phone came out, and the product became super popular. I was able to sell one hundred fifty devices a month.

On my way home, I stopped at Roscoe's House of Chicken and Waffles in Hollywood to grab a bite to eat. The group Boyz II Men were sitting at a table next to me. They noticed the phone I had. They all wanted this new phone. Nathan Morris purchased one from me, and then the rest of the group signed up. It was the phone you had to have, and Nextel was the only company that had the product.

Nathan then referred me to Halle Berry's business manager. He asked me to take over Halle's account and introduced me to all of his other clients. That opened a lot of other doors for me. I went to various movie sets to show Halle the latest products and service her account. There I was, back on the movie sets again.

Various markets surfaced for me: the movie industry, transportation, caterers, and the set crews. If one market slowed down, I would pivot to another market. It's not what you know, but who you know. And I was blessed to have a product everyone wanted at the time.

Nextel started doing product placement with Motorola. I was able to assist in getting the phones on the set and into the movies. I drove around delivering phones to celebrities like Dr. Dre, Tori Spelling, Will Arnett, Blair Underwood, Flex Alexander, and Barbara Robinson (realtor to the stars and wife of Baseball Hall of Famer Frank Robinson).

I became a trusted adviser and started to get referrals to everybody and anybody. I went to their mansions and met them on their private jets. The sky was no limit.

I wasn't chasing Hollywood, but Hollywood was chasing me. Motorola put me on the cover of a magazine with the title "Who do the Hollywood Stars turn to for Efficient Communication Technology?" I made copies of the article and stapled my business card to them. I left a copy with each client. I had learned to use every opportunity to showcase my skills and benefits.

The key was how fast you could get the information to the customer. Speed and accuracy ruled. I began to "solution sell" which was not just discussing products but also finding out what the customer's pain points were. What was hindering their business? What was keeping them from getting to the next level? I was feeling the heartbeat of the customer.

STAY HUMBLE

John Combs, President of the Nextel Southwest Area, set up a friendly business challenge with the President of the Nextel Southeast Area to determine which area of the U.S. would be considered the best. The incentive John had proposed for winning the challenge was to take the top sales representatives from the number one area to the Super Bowl in Miami by private jet. The jet was owned by Craig McCaw, who had invested over three billion dollars in Nextel. That was a lot of money.

One day John summoned me to his office and said, "Glenn, we are about five thousand units short for the month. What do we need to do to win?" I brainstormed with John and we came up with a sales promotion to meet our company goal. I was fired up and told him I'd work overtime to make it happen.

Our team sales began to skyrocket, and we won the trip to Super Bowl XXXIII in Miami, Florida. Everything was plush, and our seats were on the 50-yard line. Gloria Estefan and Stevie Wonder were the halftime show entertainment!

While gazing out of the plane window on the flight back to Los Angeles, I felt appreciation for John Combs and the entire team. We were on top of our game, and he had rewarded us for our hard work. It was a special moment, and I didn't want it to end.

I continued to receive awards and accolades, but there were challenges along the way. After receiving the Salesman of the Year award one year, as I exited the stage, a jealous sales representative accosted me and said, "You don't deserve that award!" He was drunk and spiteful.

I used this as fuel to inspire and motivate me to be the best that I could be at my craft. I reflected on my dad's words of advice, "Don't let anyone rain on your parade." These words of wisdom resonated with me and were a keepsake. It has made me the resilient person that I am today, turning negatives into positives. Not everyone is going to be happy for you when you win. And it is not just about winning, it's about winning with integrity.

Soon after that, my dad passed away from alcohol abuse and loneliness. He had a stroke and never recovered from it. He was a man with a military mind and a big heart. I returned to Peoria for my dad's funeral and received the American Flag and spent rifle casings from the twenty-one gun salute done in honor of dad's military service.

As I reflect, I wish dad had been around more when I was a kid. But the times I did spend with him were right out of a Richard Pryor movie.

I recall one time when I returned home to visit dad for Thanksgiving. He had been drinking too much and was upset. He said someone had come into his apartment and stolen his turkey and goose out of the freezer. He was so upset that he picked up the phone and called 911. He went into great detail with the person on the line, about the turkey's size and how he was planning to use the leftovers for lunch sandwiches for work the following week. He was really distraught.

I laughed so hard I had to run into the bathroom to keep from cracking up in front of him. As he reported the crime, I could hear the operator laughing, and that made my dad more upset. He gave her a piece of his mind and slammed the phone down. I told my dad, "Don't worry, I will run to McDonald's and get you a burger and fries." He said, "Stop and bring me a half pint of liquor on your way back." All I could do was shake my head as I went out the door.

URGENT CARE

One year later, I received a phone call that mom had driven her car into someone's yard on her way to church. I needed to get back to Peoria right away. I asked a person from the church to stay with mom until I could get there.

When I saw her a few days later, I could see the lupus had taken it's toll on her body and mind, and that she was not eating correctly. At that time, lupus was still being researched, and there was no cure.

I asked her doctor if I could bring mom out to California with me, and she agreed. Mom initially didn't want to leave her church and friends. I had to put on my selling cap and convince her to visit me for the winter. I said I would bring her back in the spring. Mom and I headed to the airport and landed in Los Angeles.

The doctor determined that mom needed surgery. After six months of rehabilitation, mom's nurse had enjoyed caring for her so much that she asked if she could come to the house to take care of her. She was a guardian angel who helped me Monday through Friday in the daytime. My shift was evenings and weekends. My sister and brother lived a couple hours away from me and also came to visit. Their visits would make mom very happy and give her something to look forward to.

I had to learn caregiving skills and manage my full-time job after mom arrived. She has had lupus for more than fifty years. During that time, all her good friends have passed on. After getting the proper care and best doctors, her lupus has gone into remission.

ATTITUDE IS EVERYTHING

Mom's attitude is one of positive reinforcement and faith which keeps her going. She has five doctor visits every two months, and she keeps a smile on her face even when she's having a bad day. So I made the decision to keep a positive attitude and enjoy each day.

I've dedicated this book to mom for her perseverance and strong faith. She dedicated her whole life to grandma, and I'm doing the same for her. Every day I wake up thinking of all the sacrifices she made for me. It gives me the strength to keep going no matter what and to never give up. It's all worth it in the end, especially when I see a big smile on her face each day!

After she spent the winter months with me in California, I asked mom if she was ready to go back home to Peoria. She smiled at me and said, "This is my new home!"

When mom was settled in and on her road to recovery, it was time to get back to work. It didn't take me long to get in the groove and start selling again to business accounts.

The Nextel i1000 Plus was changing things. The device had a two-way radio and cell phone built into it. The two-way radio was the hot seller. The network improved, and the cell phone portion expanded my market share from blue collar workers to white collar workers.

The new technology rejuvenated my career and was the inspiration I needed to stay on top of my game. John Combs again invited me to meet with him to focus on reaching company targets. He asked, "What do we need to do to meet our goals?"

I replied, "I think we need to focus on credit. If we can relax credit for one month, I think we can make our goals." It was harder to get credit at that time.

John agreed. He was excited that such a simple tip would help the company make its sales goals for the month and quarter. John was an incredible team player who wanted to win as much as I did and wanted to delight our customers. He admired my steady success in product sales and customer service.

A NEW CHALLENGE

Nextel opened up a new division. That's when I went into local, state, and federal government sales for four years. Sales were based on volume, possibly hundreds at a time sold, and I liked that idea.

I didn't like the sales process though — it was too slow! Speed didn't rule in this case. It could take six months to a year to close a big deal with a government agency.

It was driving me crazy having to wait. I was able to exceed my quota. But the fun part is closing the deal, and *you* don't close the government, *they* close you!

After four years, sales dried up in this area. I was looking to get back into the hustle. I decided to go back into general business. I liked the speed — how fast could I close a deal and get to the next customer! It's important to know oneself and what brings joy and energy to your everyday life.

I began to rebuild my client base and realized that many of my old clients had gone to other suppliers. Before I left to go into government sales, some of my clients had told me, "The day you leave is the day I'm gone." Well, my goal was to win them back.

In 2005 the merger happened. Sprint bought Nextel, and business opportunities increased. There was a new variety of products to sell. Instead of negatively reacting to change, I welcomed the opportunity. I could now compete on a national stage.

I was blessed to have won the President's Council award eight years in a row. John Combs had challenged me to see if I could win three. But I won eight times, which meant eight great trips: Cabo San Lucas in Mexico, Montego Bay in Jamaica, Cancun in Mexico, Nassau in the Bahamas, San Juan in Puerto Rico, Acapulco in Mexico, Maui in Hawaii. My streak ended with my second and most memorable trip to Cabo San Lucas in Mexico.

I was sitting at the awards banquet table in the front row having dinner with CEO Tim Donahue and my cousin Joe Somerville when the MC of the night came walking out and said, "Ladies and Gentlemen: Please give a round of applause to tonight's host, Mark Curry, from the TV Show 'Hangin' with Mr. Cooper'!"

My mouth fell open. I had no idea Mark was hosting. When he recognized me in the front row as his Nextel sales representative, he yelled to the lighting technician in the back to put the spotlight on the table where I sat. He asked me to come on stage, and he proceeded to roast me in front of the entire company.

"Not in front of my peers!" I thought. But then I recalled grandma's voice saying, "Stay humble." He handed me the mike and I said, "I'm just thankful to be here." That finished the roast, and I went back to my seat. It was all fun in the end. A good laugh made the night enjoyable for everyone.

I'm still having fun at this. People ask me all the time "When are you going to retire?" I tell them, "I'm just getting started."

SHE WAS THE ROCK

In 2006 grandma passed away. She lived to be 104 years old. She was the rock of the family. She helped my mother raise me and my brothers and sister. When I was a child she made sure I didn't chew gum in church. Because of her giving heart, she would replace the gum with peppermint candy.

My most memorable moment with her was walking to the bus stop to ride to downtown Peoria. I was only five years old at the time. That day she taught me that the man always walks closest to the street when he's walking with a woman. Looking back, I see Southern manners at their best in her.

I miss her pound cakes, roast beef and meatloaf. Her food always left a good taste in my mouth. And I recall grandma speaking with a southern drawl — "Aw boy, go on" — when I tried to kiss her on the cheek to compliment her on her cooking.

Grandma's spirit lives on in all of us. Right before she passed away, she told me that she was tired and ready to go home to be with the Lord. She looked forward to seeing her family together again in heaven.

My family and I attended the funeral service, honoring, and sharing memories. When we arrived at the cemetery, all of grandma's church family from Mt. Zion Baptist Church was there to greet us. It brought tears to my eyes and special memories of the past.

It is essential to honor and respect those who have made sacrifices and have contributed their wisdom along one's journey in life. And to enjoy the memories.

TURN NEGATIVES
INTO POSITIVES.

CHAPTER TWELVE

THE BIRTH OF GLENN BOWIE SPEAKS

CHAPTER TWELVE

THE BIRTH OF GLENN BOWIE SPEAKS

PRINT WAS A BLESSING AND A GIFT. IT OPENED UP DOORS FOR ME, and the momentum continues as I celebrate my thirty-first anniversary in the communication industry at the time of this writing.

I still strive to make a difference with each of my customers, and I continue to motivate myself and move forward. I like face-to-face meetings with my customers. Our interaction is my favorite part of the business. The bulk of my business is referrals, but I've always enjoyed hunting for new business as well.

My sales manager sometimes asks me to take new hires into the field to teach them. The first thing I ask them is, "What do you want out of this? What's your vision? Yes, we are here to make money, but we are really here to be of service to others and better ourselves."

SERVICE TO OTHERS

I got my first taste of motivational speaking in Phoenix, Arizona. Char Webster, Nextel Senior Marketing Manager, was there to roll out new marketing programs, and I took the journey with her. There was an audience of some fifty sales executives. As Char promoted marketing programs, I waited backstage. The anticipation gave me goosebumps. I felt an adrenaline rush. This was my first opportunity to speak to my peers. Char gave me a great introduction. She told of all my awards and accolades and commended me for integrity and perseverance in the industry.

As I approached the podium, the audience began to clap and welcomed me with open arms. I thanked them for inviting me to speak and began to speak from my heart.

I said, "One of my sales techniques is to focus on customer needs. I listen carefully to what the customer is saying, then visualize how I can make a difference in their business. It's this level of inquiry and caring that builds trust.

"Selling starts with building relationships, letting people know how important they are. You must also believe in the product and be passionate about it. People are looking for guidance. Nobody wants to be sold. They want to be happily involved."

The momentum in the room was building. The audience wrote down everything that came out of my mouth.

I was sharing my best practices: Set a goal to reach quota by the 15th of the month. Speed is key. Follow-up is critical. Go back to the basics — a firm handshake, trust-building, and find common ground.

I explained that customers would share their challenges with you if you show that you care. Then I told them to tailor their sales techniques to the customer's needs. I spoke of how valuable it is to ask questions, listen, and not talk so much. Find out what's holding a company back from meeting its goals. Research the company before you go out and visit. Go online and find out what it is about. Familiarize yourself with their mission statement and vision.

I advised them to make sure the person is listening, then speak well enough to keep them on the edge of their seats.

BACK TO THE BASICS

I told them about a time when I was in front of a customer, and he kept looking at the clock on his wall. I immediately asked him, "How are you on time?" He replied, "I have another meeting shortly. Let's move forward." I closed the deal within ten minutes.

I emphasized to my audience that it is crucial to know who the decision-maker is, and what challenges they face, to determine how you can help. I explained how much body language tells about a person. I reminded them that you must reassure the customer that you will be there for them after the sale. Try to under-promise but over-deliver.

I urged them to have the mindset to sell to the client's needs, not the needs of their own pockets. "If you don't," I said, "all of the customer's trust — that you worked so hard to get — can be lost." I told them to make sure to show the value you are adding to their business. Sometimes, you have to walk away from business if it is not a good fit.

I shared ideas on how to ask for the business. A trial close such as "How soon can you get started?" and "Can we do business today?" is useful in many cases. I also shared how to handle people who are not 100% sure. And how, after asking a closing question, you must shut up and wait. There is an art to it.

I spoke to their hearts and minds with my motivational words of wisdom, and I received a standing ovation. A gentleman from the audience stopped me as I exited the stage to tell me that I had changed his life and thanked me for sharing my expertise.

INSPIRING THE NEXT GENERATION

On the plane back from Arizona, I felt jazzed about motivational speaking. I could share my story with students in grade schools, high schools, and colleges. I could also do motivational sales presentations and training for corporations. I thought, "I want to inspire and motivate people to reach their dreams. I want to help them overcome whatever might be holding them back from achieving their goals. I have something inside of me that I can share with others."

My dreams and visions come to me when I am spending quiet time alone. They help me to focus. Then I can speak my dreams into existence. The idea of Glenn Bowie Speaks came to me in a dream in the middle of the night.

It is a God-given gift to be able to share my journey with others. I am still evolving and learning, and I know that we all have more than one gift. The sky's the limit. I want to provide a bridge between where others are and where they want to be, by sharing my successful techniques and helping others master the art of selling.

POWER OF NETWORKING

I was surprised when my next speaking engagement was for a networking event through the Los Angeles Chamber of

Commerce. Since then, I've been an Ambassador with the Los Angeles Chamber of Commerce for ten years, attending networking events and building many valuable relationships with people from all walks of life. I've found that people look to me for direction and guidance. I like inviting others into the Chamber, and for me, it has been a training ground for Glenn Bowie Speaks. Networking is key!

I was surprised to find out how shy people are. People want to meet people, but don't know how. I bridge that gap. I take their information and introduce them to whoever they want to meet. It's fun to see the energy in the room change as people make connections.

The Chamber of Commerce is where I met Victoria Franklin, who worked for the Los Angeles Job Corps. The Job Corps is a national program that helps eligible young people from ages 16 through 24 complete their high school education, trains them for meaningful careers, and assists them with obtaining employment.

Victoria was looking for a motivational speaker. "I would love to come speak to your kids," I said. I told her my story, and she was so enthused that she introduced me to Fred Williams, Executive Director at the Los Angeles Job Corps.

When I met with Fred, I shared my story with him. Fred then invited me to speak to an audience of three to four thousand people at the Los Angeles Job Corps graduation. It was my first keynote speech, and I was energized. I practiced my speech in my backyard for months, making sure it was perfect.

The students would be eager to hear what I had to say, but their attention spans would be short. I wanted to engage the audience and give them meaningful information.

I will never forget the moment when the CEO of the YWCA, Faye Washington, introduced me. Faye spoke about all of my sales experience, awards, and accolades. She mentioned how intrigued she was with my dedication to my mom's care, as she built up the audience to welcome me.

I felt like I was the king of the world. She spoke so highly of me. Her delivery and sincerity were awesome. It touched my heart and also the audience's.

As I walked up to the podium, Faye shook my hand. I felt empowered. That's when I knew I was going to make a difference in the lives of others.

I told my personal story from Peoria to California. I shared with the students what I had learned: One person can make a difference that changes your whole life. Take one day at a time, and make each minute count. Never give up. Never stop chasing your dreams.

The speech was so successful that Fred thought I had been speaking for years! It was that speech and the feedback I received from it that inspired me to write this book.

GIVING BACK

I have truly been blessed in so many ways. I stand on the shoulders of the many people who have made a difference in my personal and professional life. I am writing this book to make a difference for others in the same way. I have always been private about my life, and I don't want to come across as if I'm better than anyone else. I want to mentor each person who might take something from this book and pass it on to the next generation. I never thought thirty-one years of sales experience would get me to this point. My life is truly about making the world a better place.

I haven't always made the best choices. But even with imperfect choices, I felt I had something to share.

We all have different God-given gifts and talents. I thought I could only play sports or make sales. But I learned that when you put effort into something your confidence builds. The goal is to reach your full potential. I have always tried to focus on what I do best, building relationships with no expectations in return. I try to surround myself with positive people and energy.

Glenn Bowie Speaks (GBS) is about "speaking into existence" your dreams and goals. You can also pray, meditate, and visualize your dreams and goals when spending some quiet time alone. But however you do it, keep your dreams alive and never give up. If you fall, get back up.

Ever since I was a little kid in Peoria, coming to California was a dream for me. And here I am.

MAKE A DIFFERENCE

I want to pay it forward and give something back to the community that can impact people's lives. I want my life experiences to help others look for the right career choices and have a better future.

I returned home to Peoria in 2017 to attend the Youth Empowerment Summit. The breakout sessions on the Bradley University campus made a significant impact on the lives of many kids and even on me. Many students shared their personal stories and goals. One student suggested I should tell *my* story. This idea was validated when I met journalist Pam Adams from the Peoria *Journal Star* newspaper for lunch. We discussed many topics and then Pam said, "You're a great storyteller!" Sometimes people see things in you that you don't see in yourself.

In 2018 Cindi Reiman, the founder of Soft Skills High online curriculum, and Glenn Bowie Speaks partnered with Peoria Public School District 150 to offer students professional development courses. These courses teach employability traits and inspire participants to develop a more positive attitude, an understanding of culture, how to build a strong character, teamwork, and the ability to embrace diversity.

In 2019 I met with Faye Washington, the President and CEO of the YWCA of Greater Los Angeles, and she decided to also partner with Glenn Bowie Speaks and Soft Skills High to help the young women of the YWCA.

I was invited by the Pasadena City College Foundation to speak to the students at Pasadena City College for a "Lunch & Learn" talk in early March of 2020 on the topic "Attitude Is Everything." We discussed staying positive, goal setting, confidence, and the value of education.

I thought about when I was in college and how fast time goes by. One student pulled me aside at the end and asked for one golden nugget. I told him, "Stay strong and believe in yourself — that you can make it — and don't let anyone or anything bring you down."

KEEP IT MOVING

I'd like to see everyone take time out of their busy lives and figure out what they could do to make a difference in the world, about what impact they could have on the world.

People may have told you that you were too small to make a difference. I've been told that all my life: The baseball coach who said I wasn't fast enough to make the team. The sales trainer who told me that no one would buy from me. The jealous salesman who said I didn't deserve the award I got. And on and on.

I disagreed and pushed forward despite these people. And here I am. I made it happen! And so can you.

STRIVE TO MAKE A DIFFERENCE WITH OTHERS.

ABOUT THE AUTHOR

GLENN BOWIE HAS SPENT ALMOST THREE DECADES AS A BUSINESS SOLUTIONS CONSULTANT IN THE WIRELESS INDUSTRY. It's been a career studded with stellar accomplishments. He was one of the first to win Nextel Communications coveted President's Council Award eight times in a row. He was a Triple Crown winner at Sprint consecutively over twelve months. And he has earned over 200 sales awards to date, including a Nextel award that was named for him, "Making It Happen."

After Sprint's purchase of Nextel in 2005 Glenn contributed to the continued growth of his division as a top sales producer on Sprint's charts. Since the spring of 2020, he has become a Major Account Executive for T-Mobile, the gigantic new owner of the Sprint brand.

He volunteers at the Los Angeles Area Chamber of Commerce and has partnered with Soft Skills High Career Readiness Certificate Program—an online curriculum that teaches employability traits and inspires participants to develop a more positive attitude, which prepares students for success. He serves on the Board of Directors for the Tournament of Roses Foundation and the Pasadena City College Foundation.

The many people who have made a difference in Glenn's life have powerfully influenced him to give back through his own company, Glenn Bowie Speaks, Inc.

His company's purpose is to inspire and empower others to live happier, healthier and more productive lives. Glenn's story of how he made it out of the projects, achieving all of his goals and now enjoying the fruits of his efforts, provides testament to his approach, attitude, and beliefs. He believes one can overcome any situation in life with knowledge and drive.

His tagline is "Speaking Into Existence," and he teaches that you can do anything if you put your mind to it.

Glenn urges, "If you can take one thing from this book and make it your own, you will be on your way to accomplishing your goals."

"A LIFE IS NOT IMPORTANT EXCEPT IN THE IMPACT IT HAS ON OTHER LIVES."

— JACKIE ROBINSON